GW00818481

ECDL® 5.0

European Computer Driving Licence

Module 6 - Presentation

using PowerPoint 2003

This training, which has been approved by ECDL Foundation, includes exercise items intended to assist Candidates in their training for an ECDL Certification Programme. These exercises are not ECDL Foundation certification tests. For information about authorised Test Centres in different national territories, please refer to the ECDL Foundation website at www.ecdl.org

Release ECDL252v1

Published by:

>CiA Training Ltd
>Business & Innovation Centre
>Sunderland Enterprise Park
>Sunderland SR5 2TH
>United Kingdom

>Tel: +44 (0) 191 549 5002
>Fax: +44 (0) 191 549 9005

>E-mail: info@ciatraining.co.uk
>Web: www.ciatraining.co.uk

>**ISBN-13: 978 1 86005 678 9**

The following information applies only to candidates in Ireland.

Acknowledgements:

>The European Computer Driving Licence is operated in Ireland by ICS Skills, the training and certification body of the Irish Computer Society.
>Candidates using this courseware should register online with ICS Skills through an approved ECDL Test Centre. Without a valid registration, and the allocation of a unique ICS Skills ID number or SkillsCard, no ECDL tests can be taken and no certificate, or any other form of recognition, can be given to a candidate.

>Other ECDL Foundation Certification programmes offered by ICS Skills include Equalskills, ECDL Advanced, ECDL WebStarter, ECDL ImageMaker, EUCIP and Certified Training Professional.

>Contact: ICS Skills
>   Crescent Hall
>   Mount Street Crescent
>   Dublin 2
>   Ireland

>Website: www.ics.ie/skills
>*Email:*   *skills@ics.ie*

First published 2008

European Computer Driving Licence, ECDL, International Computer Driving Licence, ICDL, e-Citizen and related logos are all registered Trade Marks of The European Computer Driving Licence Foundation Limited ("ECDL Foundation").

CiA Training Ltd is an entity independent of ECDL Foundation and is not associated with ECDL Foundation in any manner. This courseware may be used to assist candidates to prepare for the ECDL Foundation Certification Programme as titled on the courseware. Neither ECDL Foundation nor **CiA Training Ltd** warrants that the use of this courseware publication will ensure passing of the tests for that ECDL Foundation Certification Programme. This courseware publication has been independently reviewed and approved by ECDL Foundation as covering the learning objectives for the ECDL Foundation Certification Programme.

Confirmation of this approval can be obtained by reviewing the Partners Page in the About Us Section of the website www.ecdl.org

The material contained in this courseware publication has not been reviewed for technical accuracy and does not guarantee that candidates will pass the test for the ECDL Foundation Certification Programme. Any and all assessment items and/or performance-based exercises contained in this courseware relate solely to this publication and do not constitute or imply certification by ECDL Foundation in respect of the ECDL Foundation Certification Programme or any other ECDL Foundation test. Irrespective of how the material contained in this courseware is deployed, for example in a learning management system (LMS) or a customised interface, nothing should suggest to the candidate that this material constitutes certification or can lead to certification through any other process than official ECDL Foundation certification testing.

For details on sitting a test for an ECDL Foundation certification programme, please contact your country's designated National Licensee or visit the ECDL Foundation's website at www.ecdl.org.

Candidates using this courseware must be registered with the National Operator before undertaking a test for an ECDL Foundation Certification Programme. Without a valid registration, the test(s) cannot be undertaken and no certificate, nor any other form of recognition, can be given to a candidate. Registration should be undertaken  with your country's designated National Licensee at an Approved Test Centre.

Downloading the Data Files

The data associated with these exercises must be downloaded from our website. Go to: *www.ciatraining.co.uk/data*. Follow the on screen instructions to download the appropriate data files.

By default, the data files will be downloaded to **My Documents \ CIA DATA FILES \ ECDL \ 6 Presentations**.

If you prefer, the data can be supplied on CD at an additional cost. Contact the Sales team at *info@ciatraining.co.uk*.

Aims

To demonstrate the ability to use a presentation application on a personal computer.

To understand and accomplish basic operations associated with *PowerPoint*.

Objectives

After completing the guide the user will be able to:

- Work with presentations and save them in different file formats
- Choose built in options such as the Help function within the application to enhance productivity
- Understand different presentation views and when to use them, choose different slide layouts and designs and edit slides
- Enter, edit and format text in presentations. Recognise good practice in applying unique titles to slides
- Choose, create and format charts to communicate information meaningfully
- Insert and edit pictures, images and drawn objects
- Apply animation and transition effects to presentations and check and correct presentation content before finally printing and giving presentations.

Assessment of Knowledge

At the end of this guide is a section called the **Record of Achievement Matrix**. Before the guide is started it is recommended that the user completes the matrix to measure the level of current knowledge.

Tick boxes are provided for each feature. **1** is for no knowledge, **2** some knowledge and **3** is for competent.

After working through a section, complete the matrix for that section and only when competent in all areas move on to the next section.

Contents

Section 1
Getting Started

By the end of this Section you should be able to:

Understand *PowerPoint* Principles

Start *PowerPoint*

Use the AutoContent Wizard

Recognise the Screen Layout

Understand the Menus and Toolbars

Use Help

Change Preferences

Exit *PowerPoint*

To gain an understanding of the above features, work through the **Driving Lessons** in this **Section**.

For each **Driving Lesson**, read the **Park and Read** instructions, without touching the keyboard, then work through the numbered steps of the **Manoeuvres** on the computer. Complete the **Revision Exercise(s)** at the end of the section to test your knowledge.

Driving Lesson 1 - Starting PowerPoint

▣ Park and Read

PowerPoint allows complicated and impressive presentations to be produced with ease.

The presentations can be used for on-screen shows, overhead projector shows, producing 35mm slides or for creating presentations and Web pages for use on the Internet.

They can include text in any format, pictures, organisation charts, graphs, sound and film clips, and information from the Internet. The slide show can incorporate impressive text animation and slide effects.

As well as slides, *PowerPoint* can produce presentation notes, handouts, printouts of slides and outlines of text.

There are numerous ways to start the program. The following method is recommended for beginners.

⌒ Manoeuvres

1. Starting the computer will automatically show the *Windows* **Desktop**.

2. Click once on **   start** to show the **Start** menu. All *Windows* applications can be started here.

3. Move the mouse pointer over **All Programs**. Click ▢ Microsoft Office ▸ and then ▢ Microsoft Office PowerPoint 2003 .

i   *If PowerPoint has been used recently there may be an entry for it in the **Start** menu and it can be started from there.*

4. If the **Tip of the Day** dialog box appears, click on **Close**.

i   *To close PowerPoint select **File | Exit**.*

5. The opening *PowerPoint* screen is displayed.

Driving Lesson 2 - The PowerPoint Screen

P Park and Read

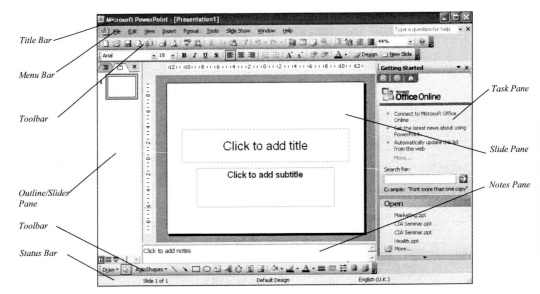

The screen should be similar to the above diagram. Work through the following manoeuvres to locate the features.

Manoeuvres

1. When certain options are selected in *PowerPoint 2003* the program tries to download content from **Office Online**, by connecting to the Internet. This can become annoying, especially for users without an Internet connection, or with a slow, dial up connection. While working through this guide, disable the option. Select **Tools | Options**, make sure the **General** tab is selected and click **Service Options**. A new window will appear; select **Online Content** from the list on the left.

2. If the **Show content and links from Microsoft Office Online** box is checked, uncheck it and click **OK**. If it is not checked, just click **OK**. Click **OK** again to close the **Options** dialog box. This change will not take effect until *PowerPoint* is restarted in a later Driving Lesson.

3. Look at the top line, the **Title Bar**, displaying **Microsoft PowerPoint**. It also shows the title of the current presentation.

Driving Lesson 2 - Continued

4.   Below that is the **Menu Bar**, where commands are chosen using the mouse.

5.   Below the menu is another bar containing two **Toolbars**. There may also be **Toolbars** at the left and bottom of the screen. Look at the buttons on these bars. They are used to access the most common menu commands.

6.   Find the bar at the bottom of the screen. This is called the **Status Bar**, where the slide number and template design will be displayed.

7.   The main part of the screen shows various views of the current presentation. The default view, shown here is **Normal View**.

8.   At the right of the screen is an area called the **Task Pane**, which provides options for performing some common tasks. It appears, disappears and changes depending on the task currently being performed. On starting *PowerPoint*, it deals with opening and creating a new presentation.

Driving Lesson 3 - Presentations

🅿 Park and Read

The *PowerPoint* **New Presentation Task Pane** offers various ways to start a new presentation.

Blank presentation provides no preset options. The user defines the layout, content and background for all slides. **Designs** can be applied later.

From design template allows the basic background design to be chosen. Individual slides and content can then be created with this background already applied.

The **From AutoContent wizard** option takes the user through the steps required to construct the content of various types of predefined presentations. All slides including backgrounds, are created and all that is required is to change the content where necessary.

From existing presentation allows an existing presentation's style and layout to be applied to a blank presentation.

Templates can also be used to create a blank presentation. *PowerPoint* has a number of templates, each with its own style, which can be opened as a blank presentation. The **on my computer** option will display the **New Presentation** dialog box. This contains a number of presentation templates. The **on my Web sites** option allows templates to be opened from a network or web server.

↱ Manoeuvres

1. If the **Office Assistant** appears at any step, right click on it and select **Hide**. This feature will be covered in a later Driving Lesson.

2. The **Getting Started Task Pane** should be displayed. Click the down arrow next to **Getting Started;** a menu will appear.

3. Take a moment to look at the menu listing all the **Task Panes** within *PowerPoint*.

4. Select **New Presentation** from the menu. Notice how the **Task Pane** changes.

Driving Lesson 3 - Continued

5.   To create a presentation using the **AutoContent Wizard**, select **From AutoContent wizard**.

6.   The **AutoContent Wizard** appears. On the left side is a diagram outlining the various stages of the wizard. Clicking on the grey square to the left of the stage name moves the wizard to that section.

7.   Click the **Next** button, 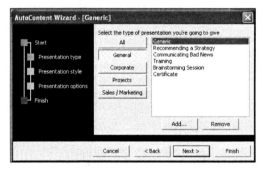, to move to the next stage.

8.   The first step is a **Presentation type**. All presentations are listed until a category is chosen from the buttons in the centre. Choose each in turn to view the presentations in the categories.

9.   From the **Sales/Marketing** category, select **Marketing Plan**, then click the **Next** button to move to the next stage.

10.   The next step is **Presentation style**. The type of output to be used is selected here. Stay with the default option of **On-screen presentation**. Click **Next**.

11.   The next step is **Presentation options**. In the **Presentation title** text box, enter the name of your company.

Driving Lesson 3 - Continued

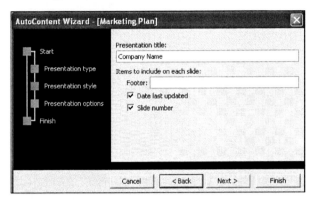

12. Remove the checks from **Date last updated** and **Slide number**, then click **Next**.

13. The wizard is now complete. Click **Finish** to view the presentation. The presentation is shown in **Normal View**.

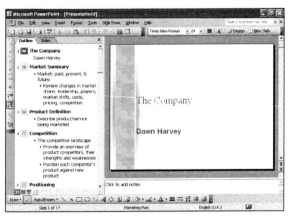

14. Notice the three distinct areas of the screen. At the left is an **Outline** view of the presentation. The main **Slide Pane** for the selected slide is shown in the right side of the screen and a small area for **Notes** appears under the **Slide Pane**.

15. Click the **Slides** tab at the top of the **Outline** view to switch that pane into **Slides** view. Using the scroll bar, view all the slides in the current presentation. The wizard has created a complete presentation with a number of slides appropriate to a **Marketing Plan**. The user can now add and remove slides and modify the contents until the required presentation is produced.

16. Keep this presentation on screen for the next few Driving Lessons.

Driving Lesson 4 - Menus

🅿 Park and Read

The **Menu Bar** contains all of the commands needed to use *PowerPoint*, within drop down lists. When *PowerPoint* starts, the **Menu Bar** displays the full range of commands. However, as they are used, the most common commands selected move to the top of the list and the rest are hidden. The hidden commands can be revealed at any time. If a command is not used for some time, it will stop appearing on the short, personalised menu.

ℹ *This customisation feature may cause the menus to look slightly different to those in this guide, but the principles remain the same.*

℞ Manoeuvres

1. Move the pointer over the word **Edit** and click with the left mouse button to open the **Edit** menu.

2. Notice how some of the commands are ghosted (very pale). This means they are not available for selection at the moment. Chevrons appear at the bottom of the list and will expand the menu if clicked on immediately. If not, the full list will appear after a few seconds. Click on **Edit** again to close the menu.

3. To use the chevrons, click on **Edit** and immediately move the mouse over the chevrons at the bottom of the drop down list to expand it.

ℹ *The menu can also be expanded by double clicking on it. If one menu is expanded, the others are expanded automatically.*

4. Close the **Edit** menu by either clicking outside the menu or click on **Edit** again. Selecting a menu option also usually closes down the menus.

5. Double click on the **Slide Show** menu to open it. Three dots after a command indicate that a further selection is available from a dialog box. Click 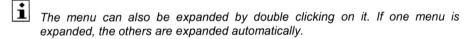 to display the **Set Up Show** dialog box.

6. Read the options available then click **Cancel** to close the dialog box.

Driving Lesson 4 - Continued

7.   Click **Tools**. If necessary, expand the menu and find **Options....** The box
     to the left of the text may be a paler shade than some of the others, which
     indicates that it is not currently part of the personalised menu.

8.   Click on **Options** to display the **Options** dialog box. After reading the
     available choices, select **Cancel** to close the dialog box.

9.   Now click **Tools** again. Notice how **Options** now appears in the short
     version of the menu. Click on **Tools** again to close the menu.

10. An arrow after a command denotes that another menu will appear. Click
     View, then hold the mouse pointer over **Toolbars**. A further menu
     appears.

11. Click on **View** again to close the menu.

12. Continue to experiment. Display the contents of the other menu options.

Driving Lesson 5 - Toolbars

🅿 Park and Read

Toolbars allow quick access to the most commonly used commands and each command is represented by a button. To save space on the screen, many buttons are hidden, but they can easily be displayed. The toolbars become personalised after being used, the frequently used buttons replacing others on the toolbar, which are then hidden.

ℹ️ *Because of this customisation feature, the toolbars may look slightly different to those in this guide, but the principles remain the same.*

🏴 Manoeuvres

1. Locate the **Toolbars**, just beneath the **Menu Bar**. The **Drawing** toolbar may also be visible at the bottom of the screen.

     Standard Toolbar   *Formatting Toolbar*

2. Move the mouse pointer over a button on the **Standard Toolbar** and leave it there for a few seconds.

3. A **ToolTip** appears, ![Save], showing the name of the button. Read the **ToolTips** for each of the visible buttons.

4. Chevrons, ■ on a toolbar indicate that there is not enough space to display all of the buttons on the toolbar. Click on the chevrons at the right of the **Standard Toolbar** or the **Formatting Toolbar** to display the toolbar options box. This shows all of the missing buttons from either toolbar.

5. Select **Add or Remove Buttons | Standard** to see all of the possible buttons which are available for the **Standard Toolbar**. Those with ticks actually appear on the toolbar (main or hidden). The **Add or Remove Buttons** feature is available on any toolbar by clicking ■.

ℹ️ *To remove a button from the toolbar, click on the tick next to it.*

6. To return toolbars to their state when *PowerPoint* was first opened for this session, select **Customize** from the **Add or Remove Buttons** list after clicking on the chevrons. Select the **Options** tab and click **Reset menu and toolbar usage data**. Select **Yes** to confirm the reset. Click **Close** to remove the dialog box.

Driving Lesson 5 - Continued

7. Toolbars can be moved so that more buttons can be seen. Click on the toolbar chevrons to display the options box again. Click **Show buttons on Two Rows.** The **Standard** and **Formatting** toolbars now have one row each and every available button can be seen.

8. To return to a single toolbar, click the arrow at the end of either toolbar to display the options. Click **Show Buttons on One Row**.

9. Select **View | Toolbars** to see the toolbars currently available. The toolbars currently in use have a tick next to them.

10. Any listed toolbar can be added to the screen by clicking on it. Click on the **Picture** toolbar to display it on the screen.

11. To remove the **Picture** toolbar from the screen, select **View | Toolbars** and click on **Picture** again.

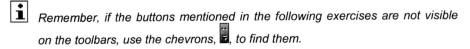 *Remember, if the buttons mentioned in the following exercises are not visible on the toolbars, use the chevrons,* ▓, *to find them.*

Driving Lesson 6 - Help

▣ Park and Read

PowerPoint includes a useful help facility with alternative ways of finding the required information using the **PowerPoint Help** task pane.

☞ Manoeuvres

1. Select **Help | Microsoft Office PowerPoint Help** to display the Help options in the Task Pane.

🛈 *If the **Office Assistant** appears when this selection is made, hide it by clicking on the **Options** button on the yellow dialog box, then selecting the **Options** tab and clicking on the **Use the Office Assistant** check box to remove the check. Click **OK**, then repeat step **1**.*

🛈 *To search for **Help** topics using Office Online the **Online Content** options must be switched on. To switch on Office Online select **Tools | Options**. Make sure the **General** tab is selected and click **Service Options**. A new window will appear. Select **Online Content** from the list on the left and check the **Show Content and Links from Office Online** and all of the check boxes below it. Click **OK** to make the changes. Click **OK** again to close the **Options** dialog box. This change will not take effect until PowerPoint is restarted.*

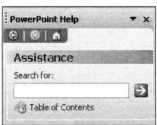

2. **Help** can be searched for in two ways. Either type in keywords into the Search box or search through the table of contents. Type **Insert** into the **Search** box and click, .

3. The search results appear in the **Task Pane**. Select **Insert a new slide** from the list. Notice that this will show the help in a new window.

4. Read the help then close the window using the **Close** button, ☒.

Driving Lesson 6 - Continued

5.   Click the **Back** button, 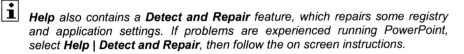, at the top of the **Task Pane**.

6.   Select **Table of Contents,** . Notice how the help topics are grouped into sections.

7.   Select **Creating Presentations** from the list. All topics associated with creating presentations will appear below, slightly indented from the main sections.

8.   Select **Create a presentation using blank slides**; a new window will appear.

9.   Read the help then close the **Help** window and close the **Task Pane**.

i   *Help* *also contains a* *Detect and Repair* *feature, which repairs some registry and application settings. If problems are experienced running PowerPoint, select* *Help | Detect and Repair*, *then follow the on screen instructions.*

Driving Lesson 7 - The Office Assistant

▣ Park and Read

PowerPoint includes another useful help facility with alternative ways of finding the required information using the **Office Assistant**.

↱ Manoeuvres

1. The **Office Assistant** provides instant on-screen help. Select **Help | Show the Office Assistant** to display the **Office Assistant**, which appears with a **What would you like to do?** dialog box.

ℹ *There are many variations of the **Office Assistant** character. The one you see may not be the one shown below. If the dialog box doesn't appear, click once on the **Office Assistant** character.*

2. In the white box, type **Toolbars** and click **Search**. A list of help options appears in the **Task Pane**.

3. Select **Create a custom toolbar** from the list of results to display the help.

4. Read the **Help**, then click the **Close** button, ▨, at the top right of the **Help** area and close the **Task Pane**.

5. If necessary, click on the **Assistant** to display the dialog box again and select **Options** from it. The **Office Assistant** dialog box appears.

Driving Lesson 7 - Continued

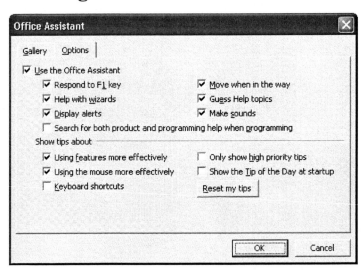

6. Options can be changed to suit individual requirements. Select the **Gallery** tab, then click the **Next** button to see another character. Keep clicking **Next** to see the characters which can represent the **Assistant**.

7. Click on the **Options** tab. Read through the available options.

8. To stop the **Assistant** appearing automatically, click on the **Use the Office Assistant** check box to remove the check.

9. Click **Cancel** to close the dialog box without changing or removing the **Assistant**.

10. Click with the right mouse button on the **Assistant** and select **Animate!** to see one of the character's animations.

11. Repeat this to see more animations.

12. Right click on the **Assistant** again and select **Hide** to remove it.

*From now on, the **Assistant** will appear whenever help is requested, unless it is disabled. At this stage, if a message about hiding the **Assistant** appears, choose to permanently turn it off.*

13. Leave the presentation open for the next Driving Lesson.

Driving Lesson 8 - Preferences

Park and Read

Basic options (**preferences**) can be changed in *PowerPoint;* for example, the default save directory. By default, documents are opened from and saved to the **My Documents** folder. This location can be changed. It is also possible to change the user name, by default, the person who installed the application is named as the user. It can be changed to show a different name, which will then appear on presentations created from templates.

Manoeuvres

1.   Click 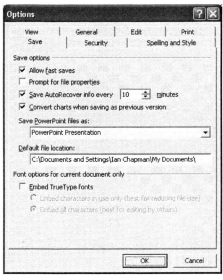 and notice that the **Look in** box in the **Open** dialog box shows **My Documents**.

2.   Click **Cancel** to close the dialog box and click ▣. The **Save As** dialog box also saves by default to **My Documents**.

3.   To change this file location, click **Cancel** to close the **Save As** dialog box, then select **Tools | Options** and click the **Save** tab.

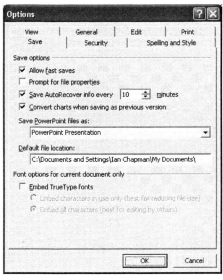

4.   In the **Default file location** box, click at the end of the existing text and add **ECIA DATA FILES\ECDL\6 Presentations**. Click **OK**. Click ▣ and notice that the new location is shown.

Driving Lesson 8 - Continued

5.   Cancel the dialog box. To change the settings back, select **Tools | Options** and the **Save** tab from the dialog box. In the **Default file location** box, amend the entry by deleting everything <u>after</u> **My Documents**, so that the location ends with **My Documents**.

6.   Click **OK**.

7.   Click **Tools | Options** and select the **General** tab from the dialog box.

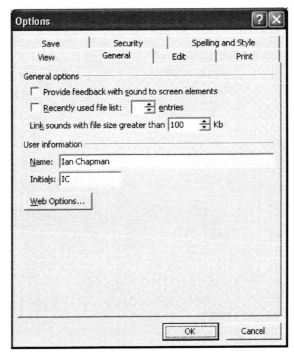

8.   Click on the box under the heading **User information** and enter your own details. This changes the **User Information** associated with the presentation.

9.   Click **OK** to apply the new settings.

*The changed settings will only be used for new presentations. The next time that a presentation is created the new name will be used. A new **AutoContent** presentation should use the new name on the title slide. For a new blank presentation, settings can be seen in the **Summary** tab in **File | Properties**.*

10.   Leave *PowerPoint* open for the next exercise.

Driving Lesson 9 - Closing PowerPoint

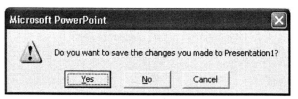 Park and Read

PowerPoint can be closed in a number of different ways, all of which are accessible from within the *PowerPoint* screen. Chose one or any number of the following ways to close the program.

Manoeuvres

1.   Select **File | Exit** to close *PowerPoint*.

If changes have been made to a recently saved presentation, or a new presentation created since the last save, a dialog box is displayed upon trying to exit the program (as shown below).

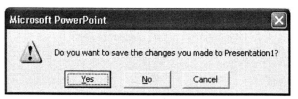

2.   Clicking **Yes** would start the **Save** process, which is covered in the next section, and then close *PowerPoint*. Clicking **No** would close *PowerPoint* without saving anything. In this instance click **Cancel**, which will cancel the close process and return to the *PowerPoint* window.

3.   Click the **Close** button [X] on the **Title Bar** (blue bar) at the top-right corner of the screen.

4.   This time click the **No** button if prompted to save the changes. *PowerPoint* will close without saving the presentation.

*Normally when closing PowerPoint with either of these actions, the **Yes** option will be taken to ensure that any important information is saved. All unsaved data will be permanently lost.*

Another method that can be used to close PowerPoint down is the key press <Alt F4>.

Driving Lesson 10 - Revision

This covers the features introduced in this section. Try not to refer to the preceding Driving Lessons while completing it.

1. Start PowerPoint.

2. Select the **AutoContent wizard** from the **New Presentation** Task Pane.

3. Select the **Financial Overview** type of presentation from the **Corporate** category.

4. Leave the default **Presentation style** as **On-screen presentation**.

5. Enter a company name in the **Presentation** title box, uncheck **Date last updated** and **Slide number** and end the **AutoContent wizard** to create the presentation.

6. What is a **toolbar**?

7. Display the **Tables and Borders** toolbar.

8. Use **ToolTips** to discover the functions of the buttons.

9. Close the toolbar.

10. Use the **Answer Wizard** from **Help** to read about printing slides. Enter **slides, printing** in the white box.

11. Read the help on the topics **Print slides** and **Print handouts**.

12. Open Creating Presentations from the Contents tab.

13. Select **Create a presentation using a design template** and read the instructions. Make sure all definitions are expanded.

14. Close the **Help** window.

15. What are preferences?

16. Open the short **Slide Show** menu.

17. How many items are shown?

18. How many items are on the full **Slide Show** menu?

19. Close *PowerPoint* selecting **No** when prompted to save.

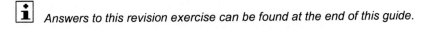 *Answers to this revision exercise can be found at the end of this guide.*

If you experienced any difficulty completing the Revision, refer back to the Driving Lessons in this section. Then redo the Revision.

Driving Lesson 11 - Revision

This covers the features introduced in this section. Try not to refer to the preceding Driving Lessons while completing it.

1.　Start *PowerPoint*.

2.　Use **Tools | Options** to change your **User Name** to **Charles Dickens**.

3.　Use the **AutoContent Wizard** to create a **Business Plan** presentation from the **Corporate** options, with a **Title** of **New Business Plan** and **Revision 10** in the **Footer**.

4.　Use **ToolTips** to discover the functions of the following buttons:

　　　a)　🖼️

　　　b)　🖨️

　　　c)　📂

　　　d)　💾

　　　e)　🗋

　　　f)　🔘

5.　Use **Tools | Options** to change your **User Name** back to your name.

6.　Close *PowerPoint* <u>without</u> saving the presentation.

ℹ️ *Answers to this revision exercise can be found at the end of this guide.*

If you experienced any difficulty completing the Revision, refer back to the Driving Lessons in this section. Then redo the Revision.

Once you are confident with the features, complete the Record of Achievement Matrix referring to the section at the end of the guide. Only when competent move on to the next Section.

Section 2
Slides & Presentations

By the end of this Section you should be able to:

Understand and Use Different Views

Understand Slide Show Basics

Save, Close and Open Presentations

Use Presentation / Design Templates

Create a Blank Presentation

Add New Slides / Insert Slides

Change Slide Layout and Background

To gain an understanding of the above features, work through the **Driving Lessons** in this **Section**.

For each **Driving Lesson**, read the **Park and Read** instructions, without touching the keyboard, then work through the numbered steps of the **Manoeuvres** on the computer. Complete the **Revision Exercise(s)** at the end of the section to test your knowledge.

Driving Lesson 12 - Views

P Park and Read

The *PowerPoint* **View** menu lists four different ways to view a presentation on screen. Each view shows a different aspect of the presentation. The views are:

Normal View	🔲	Combines the main **Slide View** with an **Outline View**, a multiple **Slides** view and an area for **Notes**. Each area of the screen can be resized individually.
Slide Sorter View	🔲	A miniature of each slide is shown. Used to order slides, add transition and animation effects (covered in later Driving Lessons).
Slide Show from current slide	🔲	Used to view presentations.
Notes Page View	🔲	Used to create presenter's notes for the slides (only available from **View** menu).

Buttons for the first three of these views are found at the lower left of most *PowerPoint* screens.

Views within the **Normal View** are:

Slide View   Used to change the text, graphics and layout of a slide and to add graphics and artwork from other applications. One slide is viewed at a time.

Outline View   Used to add or edit the presentation page titles and text. The information is shown as text only.

Slides View   List of miniature slide images with the same functions as **Slide Sorter View**. Occupies the same pane as **Outline View**, tabs are used to toggle between them.

Manoeuvres

1.   Start *PowerPoint* and use the **Autocontent wizard** to create a **Marketing Plan** presentation (**Sales/Marketing** category). Use your own company/college as the title and remove the checks from **Date last updated** and **Slide number**.

2.   **Normal View** is displayed by default. Click the **Slide Sorter View** button, 🔲. Several slides of the presentation are shown on the screen at once.

3.   Select **View | Notes Page**. The slide is shown in the top of the screen, with an area for notes at the bottom.

Driving Lesson 12 - Continued

4. Click the **Slide Show from current slide** button, ⬚. The presentation slide show starts, beginning with the slide currently being viewed.

5. Click the mouse button to go from one slide to the next. Each page is shown in turn on the screen. Continue to the end or press **<Esc>** to finish.

6. Make sure **Normal View**, ⬚, is selected and click on the **Slides** tab, ⬚ or ⬚. A list of slide miniatures is displayed with the current slide (shown in the **Slide** pane) highlighted.

7. Each pane works independently of the others, although they are also linked. Click slide **4** in the **Slides** list (use scroll bars if necessary) and slide **4** will be shown in the **Slide** pane. Click in the **Slide** pane.

8. From the menu, select **View | Zoom** and choose **100%** from the **Zoom** dialog box. Click **OK** (a slide miniature may appear).

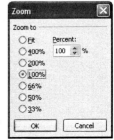

9. Use the scroll bar at the bottom of the **Slide** pane to see more of the slide.

10. Now click on the drop down arrow of the **Zoom** box on the **Standard Toolbar** and select **Fit** from the list. The slide returns to its dimensions when *PowerPoint* was originally opened.

11. Select the **Outline** tab, ⬚ to show the contents of the slides in the left pane. Each slide is represented by a small icon and the slide number, ¹⬚.

12. Use the scroll bar at the right of the pane to display slide **10**. Move the mouse over the icon until it becomes ⬚. Click once to display slide **10** in the **Slide** pane. The associated text and icon are highlighted in the **Outline** pane.

13. Move the mouse over the border at the right of the **Outline** pane until it becomes ⬚. Click and drag to change the size of the pane until it fills about half the screen. Drag to the left to decrease the size of the pane or to the right to increase it. Drag the border back to its original position.

14. View slide 4, Competition. Click in the Notes pane and type in Sales Director to give brief report on our competitors.

ℹ️ *If graphics are required in notes, they must be inserted in **Notes Page View**.*

15. Practise moving between slides and leave the presentation on screen for the next Driving Lesson.

Driving Lesson 13 - Slide View

P Park and Read

Slide View - the pane at the right within **Normal View** - shows the presentation slides, one at a time, with all text properly formatted and with a background template. This is the main area used to create, edit and format most slide content.

The scroll bar at the right of the screen can be used to move from one slide to another.

In all the views except **Slide Show**, pressing <**Ctrl Home**> or <**Ctrl End**> moves directly to the first or last slide in a presentation respectively.

Manoeuvres

1. With the presentation created earlier still on screen, ensure **Normal View** is selected and increase the size of the main **Slide** pane by clicking and dragging the dividing border to the left.

2. Click on the **Next Slide** button, ⬇, to move to the next slide.

3. Click on the **Previous Slide** button, ⬆, to move back one slide.

4. Click and drag the scroll button up or down the scroll bar, as appropriate. Release the mouse button when the marker for the sixth slide, **Communication Strategies,** appears.

> Slide: 6 of 17
> Communication Strategies

5. Press <**Ctrl End**> to move to the last slide in the presentation.

6. Press <**Ctrl Home**> to move to the first slide in the presentation.

7. Practise moving through the slides in **Normal View**, then return to **Slide 1**.

Driving Lesson 14 - Outline View

▣ Park and Read

Outline View shows all of the text used in a presentation, without any slide formatting or background patterns. The text is shown as a list, with the slide titles in bold. The slide number is shown in the left margin, with a slide icon, ▣ , at the left of the title text. This view makes it easy to manipulate text between slides. To add text in **Outline View**, click on the icon ▣ representing the required slide and proceed to type in the text. The **Promote** and **Demote** buttons can be used to change the text from a title, to a subtitle, and back again.

> 2 ▣ **This is a Slide Title**
> • This is demoted text
>   • This is further demoted

There are various buttons at the left of the screen that are used in **Outline View** to move and arrange slides. Some of the buttons are:

◄	Promote the selected text
►	Demote the selected text
▲	Move the selected text up the list
▼	Move the selected text down the list
▬	Collapse (Show slide title only)
＋	Expand (Show slide title and contents)
▀≣	Collapse all slides
↓≣	Expand all slides
▤	Summarise slides
ᴬ⁄A	Show formatting of text

☞ Manoeuvres

1. Using the current presentation, switch to **Normal View** and select the **Outline** tab on the right. If the above buttons are not visible, select **View | Toolbars | Outlining**.

2. In the left margin, click on slide **6**. All the text for that slide is now selected. Expand the **Outline Pane** if necessary.

Driving Lesson 14 - Continued

3. Move the mouse pointer to the left of **Messaging by audience**, underneath the title **Communication Strategies**. The mouse pointer changes to a ⬥. Click the mouse once. The text for that point is selected.

4. Click the **Move Down** button, ⬛. The line of text moves down the list by one line.

5. With the text still selected, click the **Move Up** button, ⬛, to put the text back in its original position.

6. With the line of text still selected, move the mouse pointer to the left of the text until the pointer is a ⬥. Click and drag downwards. As the mouse pointer is moved down, a line appears across the screen. When the line is just below **Target consumer demographics**, release the mouse button. The text will move to the new position. Drag the text back to its original position.

ℹ️ *Text can also be moved between slides in this way.*

7. It is easy to edit text in this view. Select slide **4 Competition** and click after **landscape**. Press the spacebar and type in **today**. Notice how the text in the main slide area changes too.

8. Select all the text for the **Title slide**, slide number **1**, by clicking once on the slide icon, ⬛.

9. Click the **Collapse** button, ⬛, to see just the title for this slide.

10. Notice that the title is now underlined, showing it is collapsed.

11. With the title still highlighted, click on the **Expand** button, ⬛, to restore the text for that slide.

12. Click the **Collapse All** button, ⬛, to see just the slide titles.

13. Click the **Expand All** button, ⬛, to show all the slide text.

14. Click the **Show Formatting** button, ⬛, to remove the slide formatting from the text in the left pane.

15. Click the button again to restore the formatting.

Driving Lesson 15 - Slide Sorter View

🅿 Park and Read

Slide Sorter View shows a thumbnail of slides in a presentation on screen. This makes it easy to move, add or delete slides and to decide on animated transitions (special effects, e.g. fade or dissolve) for moving from slide to slide. Transitions and effects are covered in later Driving Lessons.

⤵ Manoeuvres

1. With the presentation still on screen, switch to **Slide Sorter View**. The screen will appear similar to below. Use the **Zoom Control**, 66%　▾, to display more or fewer slides (fewer slides will be shown if the screen resolution is below 800x600).

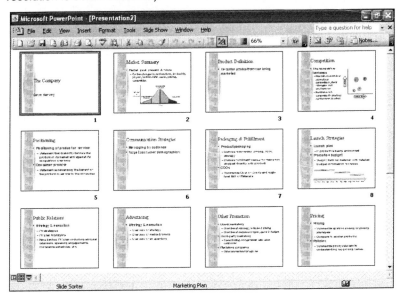

2. Click the **Show Formatting** button, (now at the top of the screen), to switch the formatting off. The slides will now show only their titles. Click the button again to restore the normal view.

3. Click on the middle of slide number **3**, hold down the left mouse button and move it about the screen. Notice that as the mouse pointer moves about the screen, a faint grey line appears, moving between slides. When the mouse button is released, the line is replaced by the slide.

4. Release the mouse button when the line is between slides **5** and **6**. The **Product Definition** slide has now become slide **5**.

Driving Lesson 16 - Notes Page View

▣ Park and Read

Notes Page View allows presenter's notes to be added to slides. The top of the screen shows the slide and lower part is reserved for presenter's notes. The scroll bar and buttons at the right edge of the screen can be used to move from one page to another.

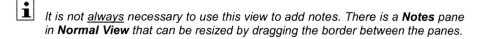 *It is not <u>always</u> necessary to use this view to add notes. There is a **Notes** pane in **Normal View** that can be resized by dragging the border between the panes.*

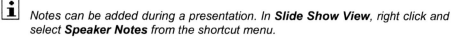 *Notes can be added during a presentation. In **Slide Show View**, right click and select **Speaker Notes** from the shortcut menu.*

↱ Manoeuvres

1. Using the current presentation, select **View | Notes Page**.

2. Use the scroll bar, if necessary, to move to the notes for slide **5**.

3. Click on the **Zoom** button on the **Toolbar** and choose **100%** from the drop down list.

4. The bottom half of the page should now be visible, with the words **Click to add text**. If this notes area is not visible, try scrolling the page up and down using the scroll bar.

5. Click on the words **Click to add text**. The words disappear and the box is highlighted. Type the following note:

    This is a notes page. Speaker's notes can be added here so that the presenter knows what to say when this slide is being shown.

6. Click on the white space outside the notes area to finish entering the text. Zoom to **50%** to see the whole page.

7. Move to slide **1** and switch to **Normal View**.

8. Click in the **Notes** pane and add the following note, zooming in if necessary:

    This is the first slide.

9. Switch to **Notes Page View** to confirm that the note is there.

Driving Lesson 17 - Slide Show

▣ Park and Read

Slide Show is used to view slides, one at a time, as an on screen presentation. This gives the creator an opportunity to view the presentation as others will see it. It is particularly useful in viewing the full effect of animations and transitions.

While the slide show is in progress, the mouse can be used to draw on the slide to highlight key points and notes can be added to individual slides.

↱ Manoeuvres

1. Using the presentation from the previous Driving Lesson, select **View | Slide Show**. The slide show starts, with the first slide filling the screen.

2. Click the left mouse button or press <**Page Down**> to move to the next slide.

3. To move back to the first slide, press <**Page Up**> or click the right mouse button and select **Previous** from the shortcut menu.

4. To move to a non-adjacent slide, click the right mouse button and select **Go to Slide** from the shortcut menu. Select **10 Advertising** and that slide will be displayed.

ℹ️ *The shortcut menu can also be displayed by clicking the popup menu button,*

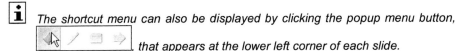 *, that appears at the lower left corner of each slide.*

5. Display the shortcut menu (using the method shown in the note above) and click the pointer button. This displays the **Pointer Menu**. Select **Ballpoint Pen** from the menu. The mouse pointer changes into a small dot.

6. Move the pen on to the slide and click and drag. The pointer draws a line on the slide. All lines drawn with any pen are saved to the presentation. Select **Erase All Ink on Slide** from the **Pointer Menu** to delete the lines drawn.

7. Display the **Pointer Menu** again this time select **Arrow** to return the mouse pointer to normal. View the rest of the presentation. When the end of the show is reached, a black screen appears, with the words **End of slide show, click to exit.**

ℹ️ *If this black screen does not appear, select **Tools | Options** and click the **View** tab. Select the **End with black slide** option, click **OK** and view the show again.*

8. Click once to return to the last view used.

Driving Lesson 18 - Saving a Presentation

▣ Park and Read

A presentation must be saved if it is to be used again. There are two main ways to save: **Save** to save a new presentation or to update changes made to an existing one, **Save As** to save a presentation under a new name, or to a different location or in a different format.

⤺ Manoeuvres

1.   The presentation created earlier is now going to be saved. Make sure that the data files for this module have been downloaded (see **Downloading the Data Files** on page 3). The data by default is stored in the folder **My Documents\CIA DATA FILES\ECDL\6 Presentations**.

2.   Select **File | Save** from the **Menu Bar** (the **Save** button, or the key press **<Ctrl S>**, can also be used).

3.   From the dialog box, choose **My Documents** from the **Places Bar** (if not already there by default).

4.   Double click **CIA DATA FILES**, then **ECDL**, and finally **6 Presentations**.

5.   In the **File name** box, type **My Product**, replacing any existing text.

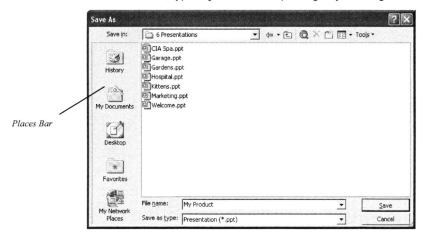

6.   Click on the drop down arrow at the right of the **Save as type** box to see the different formats available, including: text format **Outline/RTF** (*.rtf), **Design Template** (*.pot), earlier versions of *PowerPoint*, e.g. **PowerPoint 95** (*.ppt), graphics formats including **JPEG File** (*.jpg) and **Windows Metafile** (*wmf).

Driving Lesson 18 - Continued

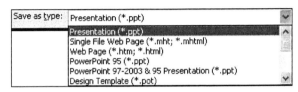

7.   Choose the default format **Presentation** (*.ppt).

8.   Click the **Save** button, [**Save**   ].

9.   To save the presentation in a different format, or another name, select **File | Save As**.

10.   The presentation is to be saved as an **Outline** file. This means that a presentation saved as an **rtf (Rich Text Format)** outline can be opened in various programs such as *Word*, although any graphic content will be lost.

11.   Change the File name to My Outline and from **Save as type** select Outline/RTF(*.rtf), then click Save.

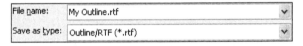

12.   To make sure that the file has been saved correctly, click the **Open** button, [icon], make sure the location where your files are saved is selected and change **Files of type** to **All Files (*.*)**.

13.   The **Outline** file should appear as [icon]My Outline.rtf. This icon indicates that only the text has been saved.

14.   Click the **Cancel** button to close the **Open** dialog box.

15.   A presentation can be saved in a special format - a **PowerPoint Show** - that allows people who don't have *PowerPoint* installed to view it. Select **File | Save As** and change the **File name** to **My Show**. From **Save as type** select **PowerPoint Show (*.pps)** and click **Save**.

16.   Repeat step 12 and notice the file icon, [icon]My Show.pps. Close the **Open** dialog box.

[i] *Remember that files can be saved to any folder or to a particular folder that you have been instructed to use.*

[i] *To be able to post a presentation to the World Wide Web, select **File | Save as Web Page** to save the presentation in the correct format.*

Driving Lesson 19 - Closing a Presentation

🅿 Park and Read

To clear the screen and begin working on a new presentation, the current one can be closed. If the presentation has not been previously saved, or if it has been modified in any way, a prompt to save it will appear.

Manoeuvres

1. With the presentation from the previous Driving Lesson on screen, select **File | Close**.

2. If no changes to the presentation have been made since it was saved in the previous Driving Lesson the presentation will close immediately.

3. If any further changes have been made to the presentation, there will be a message asking if the new version of the presentation is to be saved, e.g. **Do you want to save the changes you made to My Product.ppt?** Click on **No**. The presentation now closes without saving.

4. A blank *PowerPoint* screen is now shown, ready to start a new presentation, open an existing one or close *PowerPoint*.

Driving Lesson 20 - Opening Presentations

▣ Park and Read

Once created and saved, a presentation can be opened at any time.

↪ Manoeuvres

1.   Click the **Open** button, 🖆. This displays the **Open** dialog box.

ℹ *Alternatively, use either **File | Open** menu or the key press **<Ctrl O>**.*

2.   Check that the **Look in** box displays the **6 Presentations** folder, if not, click on **My Documents** from the **Places Bar** to view the contents of that folder, then navigate to the **6 Presentations** folder.

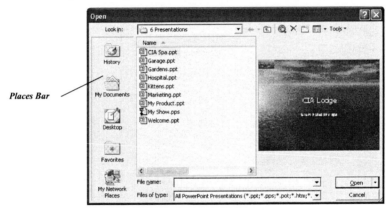

3.   The **My Product** presentation should be listed. Click on it once to select it, then click on ⎣ **Open** ▾⎦ to open the presentation.

4.   Move to the **Notes** page for slide **5**. Use zoom if necessary to see the text. Change **This is a notes page** to **This is an interesting notes page**.

5.   Because the presentation has been changed, a copy of the original is required as well, use **File | Save As** to save the presentation as **My Product2**, and leave it open.

6.   Now open the two presentations called **Hospital** and **Gardens**, which should also be in this folder, using the **Open** button.

7.   Change between the open presentations by clicking on their button in the **Taskbar**.

8.   Practise switching between the presentations, then close all the presentations <u>without</u> saving.

Driving Lesson 21 - New Presentations

P Park and Read

When creating a new presentation with a **Blank Presentation** template, all that has to be specified is the type of slide to be used, i.e. Title slide, bulleted text, etc. A blank slide will be produced, without colours, background, graphics, etc.

☞ Manoeuvres

1.   Select **File | New** to display the **New Presentation** task pane.

2.   Under **New**, click **Blank presentation** to start a new, blank presentation.

3.   The **Slide Layout Task Pane** appears on the right of a **Normal View** screen. The first layout **Title Slide** should be selected by default, Click on a few other layouts to see how the view in the **Slide** pane changes. Finally, click on the **Title Slide** layout again.

4.   A completely blank presentation slide has been created. Text can be added to the boxes as indicated.

5.   Switch to each of the different views in turn to see the effect. From this position, any aspect of the presentation can be defined.

6.   **Close** the presentation without saving.

i   *Usually, all presentations start with a **Title Slide** to introduce the presentation.*

Driving Lesson 22 - Creating a Presentation

Park and Read

A variety of ways to create and view a presentation have now been examined. From this onwards, a presentation will be created using the major features of *PowerPoint*. Design templates provide a common style throughout a presentation. This includes a common background, and related colours for text and graphics.

Manoeuvres

1. Select **File | New**.

2. At the **New Presentation** task pane, click on the **From design template** link.

3. From the list of designs, select a few to see how they appear in the **Slide** pane. Finally select the design **Ocean** (they are in alphabetical order and **ToolTips** appear when the mouse is held over a design).

4. The first (**Title**) slide in the presentation has now been created with the **Ocean** design applied. Notice how the **Status Bar** shows **Slide 1 of 1**.

5. Make sure **Normal View** is selected.

6. On the **Title Slide** of the new presentation, click on the area **Click to add title** and type the title **CIA Training Ltd**.

7. Click on the **Click to add subtitle** area and type **A PowerPoint Presentation**.

 *If it is not possible to complete the remainder of the guide in one session, then save the presentation, at any time, as **CIA**, and continue at a later date.*

Driving Lesson 23 - Adding and Deleting Slides

Park and Read

A new slide can be added to a presentation at any time. New slides are placed directly after the slide that is currently selected. If necessary, their position can easily be changed later using the **Slides** pane or **Slide Sorter View**.

Make sure that each slide has a different title. This makes it much easier to navigate between slides in **Slide Show View**, or to distinguish between slides in **Outline View** or other views. It's also good practice to be concise when entering text on slides, e.g. use short phrases and bullet points or numbered lists instead of long sentences. The idea of a presentation is that you expand on these brief points when delivering it.

Manoeuvres

1. Click the **New Slide** button, New Slide.

2. In the **Slide Layout** task pane, place the cursor over each layout, read the tooltip. **Title Slide** and the **Title Only** layouts are often used to start presentations. Other formats are used to display content.

3. Click on the second layout, **Title only**. A new slide, number **2**, has now been created. The **Status Bar** now shows **Slide 2 of 2**.

4. Use the **New Slide** button to create a new slide after slide **2**, using the **Title and 2-Column Text** layout. The **Status Bar** now shows **Slide 3 of 3**

To position a new slide in a particular place, click between the required slides in Slides View or Slide Sorter View and then insert the new slide.

5. On slide **3**, click to add the title **Presentation Agenda**. Notice the handles around the text. These can be used to resize the text area.

6. Click at the top of the first column of text and type **The Company**. Press <**Enter**> and type **The People**. On the next line, type **The Products**.

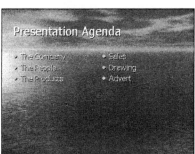

7. In the second column of text, enter **Sales** on the first line, **Drawing** on the second and **Advert** on the third line.

8. Select slide **2** by clicking on it in the **Slides Pane**, the select **Edit | Delete Slide** or press the <**Delete**> key. The slide is removed.

9. **Save** the presentation as **CIA** and leave it open.

Driving Lesson 24 - Changing Slide Layout

▣ Park and Read

The layout of a slide can be changed after it has been added to a presentation.

ℝ Manoeuvres

1. On slide **2 Presentation Agenda**, click and drag the mouse over the text in the left column to highlight it and then press **<Delete>**.

2. Repeat this for the text in the right column.

3. To change the type of slide, select **Format | Slide Layout**.

4. From the **Slide Layout** task pane, select the **Title and Table** layout from the **Other Layouts** section.

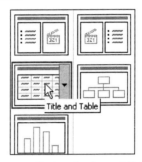

5. Double click the table icon to display the **Insert Table** dialog box.

6. Change the value in the **Number of rows** box to **3**.

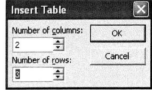

7. Click **OK** to create the table, then with the cursor in the first cell type **The Company**.

8. On second thoughts, a bulleted list would be more appropriate. Highlight **The Company** and press **<Delete>**. Click exactly on the table border (the pointer becomes a four headed arrow) and press **<Delete>** to remove the table.

9. The **Slide Layout Task Pane** should still be displayed, select the **Title and 2-Column Text** layout.

10. Retype the original text - the picture on the previous page should help.

11. Save the presentation and leave it open.

Driving Lesson 25 - Background Colour

Park and Read

The background colour of specific slides or all slides can be changed. However, it is preferable not to use too many different colours in the same presentation.

Manoeuvres

1. In **Normal View**, add two new slides, both **Title and Text** layout, after slide **2**.

2. Switch to **Slide Sorter View** and select slide **3**.

3. Select **Format | Background** and from the drop down list at the bottom of the dialog box. Select **More Colors**.

4. Select the **Standard** tab from the **Colors** dialog box. Select a vivid **pink** from the honeycomb.

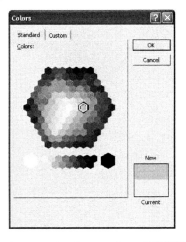

5. Click **OK**. To apply the new background to slide **3** only click **Apply** (**Apply to All** would change the colour of all slides).

6. In the same way, select slide **4** and change its background colour to yellow.

7. Delete slide **4** by making sure it is selected and then pressing <**Delete**>.

8. Delete slide **3** and close the presentation, saving the changes.

Driving Lesson 26 - Revision

This covers the features introduced in this section. Try not to refer to the preceding Driving Lessons while completing it.

1.   Create a **New Blank Presentation** selecting the **Title Slide** layout.

2.   Click on the title slide and add title text **Put Your IT Skills to the Test**.

3.   Click to add the Subtitle 'by Your Name'.

4.   Insert a **New Slide** using the **Title and Text** layout.

5.   Click to add the title **Introduction**.

6.   Click to add the following bullet points:

- **Concepts of ICT**
- **Using the computer and managing files**
- **Word processing**
- **Spreadsheets**
- **Using databases**
- **Presentation**
- **Web browsing and communication**

7.   Save the file naming it **IT Skills**.

8.   Close the presentation.

If you experienced any difficulty completing the Revision, refer back to the Driving Lessons in this section. Then redo the Revision.

Driving Lesson 27 - Revision

This covers the features introduced in this section. Try not to refer to the preceding Driving Lessons while completing it.

1.   Open the presentation **CIA Spa**.

2.   View the notes page for the first slide.

3.   Use the **zoom** control to change the magnification of the page to **100%**.

4.   Insert the following text into the notes page area.

> **Good Morning Ladies and Gentlemen, welcome to CiA Lodge.**
>
> **I am (your name) and I will be your speaker for this presentation.**
>
> **First of all I would like to give you a brief introduction to the business.**

5.   Use the zoom control to display the whole page.

6.   Change to **Slide Sorter View** and select slide **2**.

7.   Display the slide in **Notes Page View** and insert the following text:

> **Since 1985 CiA Lodge has been a successful hotel and spa.**
>
> **Every treatment is uniquely customised to our guests' requirements. Our aim is to ensure that each guest receives the benefit of personal attention. Our philosophy has resulted in many repeat bookings and a regular clientele.**

8.   Make sure the option is set to end the presentation with a black end slide. Switch to **Slide Show View**.

9.   View the whole show.

10.   Save the presentation as **CIA Lodge**.

11.   Close the presentation.

If you experienced any difficulty completing the Revision, refer back to the Driving Lessons in this section. Then redo the Revision.

Once you are confident with the features, complete the Record of Achievement Matrix referring to the section at the end of the guide. Only when competent move on to the next Section.

Section 3
Formatting

By the end of this Section you should be able to:

Apply Formatting, Text Effects and Bullets

Use Undo and Redo

Change Alignment and Spacing

Use Cut, Copy and Paste

Use Animation Schemes and Custom Animation

Apply Headers & Footers

Work with Master Pages

Check Spelling

To gain an understanding of the above features, work through the **Driving Lessons** in this **Section**.

For each **Driving Lesson**, read the **Park and Read** instructions, without touching the keyboard, then work through the numbered steps of the **Manoeuvres** on the computer. Complete the **Revision Exercise(s)** at the end of the section to test your knowledge.

Driving Lesson 28 - Formatting: Font & Size

![P] Park and Read

The text on any slide can be formatted in a number of ways, including changing the font, size, appearance, colour, alignment, etc. Many of the normal features of word processing are available when entering or editing text on a slide.

Manoeuvres

1. Open the **CIA** presentation and view the **Presentation Agenda** slide in **Normal View**.

2. Click and drag the mouse over the text in the first column to select it.

3. Click on the **Font** drop down arrow, `Tahoma` ▾ and choose a different font from the list.

4. Using the **Font Size** button, `28 ▾`, choose a larger size of font.

5. Click on the **Increase Font Size** button, **A⌃**.

6. If necessary, change the font size so that each item in the column is at its maximum size but still fits on one line.

7. With the text still highlighted, select **Format | Font** to display the dialog box (the **Font** dialog box will probably have different selections made).

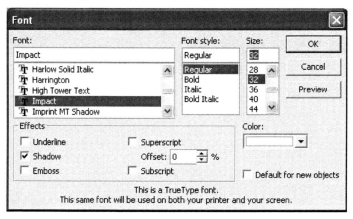

8. Choose the **Arial Black** font and size **28** from the dialog box and click **OK**.

9. Leave the presentation open.

Driving Lesson 29 - Undo and Redo

▣ Park and Read

The **Undo** and **Redo** functions can be really useful, for example if something is deleted by mistake the deletion can be undone. **Undo** cancels the last action performed and **Redo** cancels the **Undo** action, leaving the presentation as it was originally.

↷ Manoeuvres

1. Viewing the **Presentation Agenda** slide of the **CIA** presentation, select the text in the second column.

2. Press **<Delete>**.

3. To replace the deleted text, select **Edit | Undo Clear**.

ℹ *The wording after **Undo** and **Redo** changes depending on the action last performed.*

4. To delete the text again, select **Edit | Redo Clear**.

5. Click **Undo**, , to replace the text.

6. Click the drop down arrow at the right of the **Undo** button, to see all of the actions that could be reversed.

7. Click **Redo**, , to remove the text again.

8. **Undo** the deletion.

9. Leave the presentation open.

Driving Lesson 30 - Applying Text Effects

Park and Read

Various effects such as bold, italic, underline and shadow can be applied to selected text on a presentation slide. Text colour can also be changed.

Manoeuvres

1. Using the **Presentation Agenda** slide, select the text in the first column.

2. Click the **Bold** button, **B**, to see the effect. Try the **Italic**, **I**, and **Underline**, **U**, in turn. Shadow is already applied, click **Shadow**, **S**, to remove it. Reapply the shadow by clicking **S**.

3. Remove all the effects except the shadow when finished.

4. Text can be offset from its normal position using subscript and superscript. Add a new **Title and Text** slide and add the title **Text Effects**.

5. For the first bullet, type **CIATM** and for the second bullet type **H2O**. Select the letters **TM** from the first bullet, then select **Format | Font** and check the **Superscript** box then click **OK**.

6. Notice how a "trademark" symbol has been created. Now select the **2** from the second bullet and display the **Font** dialog box again, this time selecting **Subscript** before clicking **OK**.

7. Select all of the text. Click the drop down arrow on the **Font Colour** button, **A ▾**, also found on the **Drawing** toolbar at the bottom of the screen. The colour box appears.

i *If the **Drawing** toolbar is not visible, select **View | Toolbars | Drawing**.*

8. The colours already used or pre-defined as appropriate to this background are shown. Select any available colour or click **More Colors** to choose a new colour from the honeycomb, then click **OK**.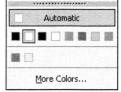

9. With the text still selected, select **Format | Font**. Select any effects and colours desired. Click **OK** to see the effect. Note that some effects cannot be seen properly while the text is still selected.

i *Text cannot be both **Embossed** and **Shadowed**, nor **Superscript** and **Subscript**.*

10. Delete this slide from the presentation by switching to **Slide Sorter View**, ensuring the **Text Effects** slide is selected and pressing <**Delete**>.

Driving Lesson 31 - Alignment, Spacing & Case

🅿 Park and Read

Alignment of the text, spacing and case can be altered to suit the user. Spacing out the text can sometimes make it easier to read.

☞ Manoeuvres

1. Using the **Presentation Agenda** slide of the **CIA** presentation in **Normal View**, select all the text in the first column.

2. Click the **Center** button, ▣ and then the **Align Left** button, ▣, to see the difference.

3. Select **Format | Alignment | Align Right**. Try choosing other alignments from the menu, before reverting back to **Left** aligned.

4. Text can also be aligned vertically in a text box. Click on the left text box and select **Format | Placeholder**. Select the **Text Box** tab and drop the **Text anchor point** list down to display the available options.

5. Select **Bottom** and click **OK** to anchor the text to the bottom of the box. Click the **Undo** button to revert the alignment to the **Top** (the default).

6. Select all the text in the box then select **Format | Line Spacing**. The dialog box appears.

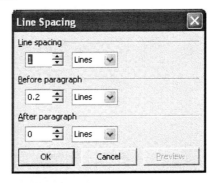

7. Change the **Line Spacing** to **2** lines, either by typing in the box or clicking on the up arrow button until the spacing reads **2**.

8. Click **OK**. The lines of text are now double spaced.

Driving Lesson 31 - Continued

9. Change the line spacing back to **1**.

10. Change the spacing both **Before** and **After paragraph** to **0.5 Lines** by typing in the appropriate boxes.

11. Click **OK** and notice the difference in how the text is spaced compared to the other column.

12. With the text in the second column selected, choose **Format | Change Case**.

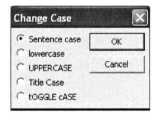

13. Select **UPPERCASE | OK**. The text will now be all in upper case.

14. Select **Format | Change Case | lowercase | OK**.

15. Select **Format | Change Case | Title Case | OK**. The text is back to its original format.

16. Practise changing the alignment and spacing.

17. Change the text in both columns back to normal (left aligned, single line spacing, **0.2** lines before paragraph and **0** lines after paragraph).

Driving Lesson 32 - Bullets

▣ Park and Read

Text in a list is usually **bulleted**; the type, colour and size of the bullet can be changed. Bullets can also be selected from a grid containing all the symbol characters associated with different fonts.

⟱ Manoeuvres

1. With the text in the first column of the **Presentation Agenda** slide selected, click the **Bullets** button, ▦, to remove the bullets. Click the button again to reapply them.

2. Bulleted text can also have an indent applied to move it further to the right. Select the text in the first column and click **Increase Indent**, ▦.

3. With the text still selected, click **Decrease Indent**, ▦, to remove the indent.

4. Select **Format | Bullets and Numbering**. The **Bullets and Numbering** dialog box appears.

5. Choose a different bullet from the options, select a different colour and size, then click **OK**.

6. The bullets have changed. Select **Format | Bullets and Numbering** again and practise changing bullet types by clicking the **Customize** button and selecting various characters from the grid. Different fonts can be displayed using the **Font** drop down list.

7. With the first column of text selected, display the **Bullets and Numbering** dialog box and select the **Numbered** tab. To number the text, select any **1,2,3** option (an example is shown opposite) and click **OK**.

8. Change the numbering to lower case Roman numerals, i.e. **i,ii,iii**.

9. Now reapply any bullet style to the first column of bullets.

10. Once the bullets in the first column have been changed, apply the same bullet style and text formatting to the second column and leave the presentation open.

Driving Lesson 33 - Cut & Paste

▣ Park and Read

The **Cut** and **Paste** commands allow text and other items, such as graphics or slides to be moved around a presentation from one place to another, quickly and easily. When an item is cut, it is removed from its original location.

When copied or cut, the item is placed in a temporary storage area known as the **Clipboard**. Up to **24** cut or copied items can be held on the **Clipboard**, which is common to all *Windows* applications.

⮡ Manoeuvres

1.   Select **Edit | Office Clipboard** to display the **Clipboard** task pane. If it contains any items, click ▧ Clear All to delete them.

ℹ️ *If any **Task Pane** is displayed, the **Clipboard** can be selected by clicking the **Other Task Panes** drop down arrow at the top right of the pane and selecting **Clipboard**.*

2.   Position the cursor in the first line of text on the **Presentation Agenda** slide - **The Company**. Select the word **The**, press the **<Delete>** key to delete the word and then type in **Our**. Add a space if necessary.

3.   Select the first line of text, **Our Company**. Make sure the selection includes the space after the text.

4.   Click on the **Cut** button, ✂, and the text is removed from the slide and placed on the **Clipboard**, where it is represented by an icon.

ℹ️ *Alternatively use the **Edit | Cut** menu or the key press **<Ctrl X>** to cut items and place them in the **Clipboard**.*

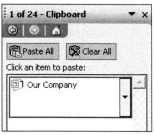

5.   Place the cursor at the end of **The Products** and press **<Enter>** to create a new bullet and empty line. Click on the icon from the **Clipboard** to paste the text at the new location.

Driving Lesson 33 - Continued

6.   If the text being pasted has a different format to its target location, a **Smart Tag** called **Paste Options** will be displayed, 📋. Click the **Smart Tag** to see the options.

7.   Select the **Keep Source Formatting** to ensure that the pasted text keeps the formatting it had when it was cut or copied.

> ℹ️ *Bullets can pose problems when cutting and pasting. Sometimes blank bullet lines are left behind or created during the process. Press <**Backspace**> when on an empty line to remove the line and the bullet.*

8.   Click and drag to select the line **The People** and cut it using any method.

9.   Open the **My Product2** presentation in **Normal View** and move to slide **5 Product Definition**.

10.   Place the cursor at the end of **marketed** and press <**Enter**>.

11.   Click the icon on the **Clipboard** to paste the text **The People** from the **CIA** presentation.

12.   Click the **Smart Tag** to see the paste options and select **Keep Text Only** to ensure that the pasted text takes on the formatting of existing text.

> ℹ️ *Selecting **Use Design Template Formatting** will ensure that the pasted text takes on the default formatting of the target slide.*

13.   Change to **Slide Sorter View** and click on slide 10. Now click on the **Cut** button and the slide disappears.

> ℹ️ *If the **Clipboard** is not being viewed, the **Paste** button, 📋, the **Edit |Paste** menu or the key press <**Ctrl V**> can be used to paste the* last *item cut or copied.*

14.   To reposition the removed slide, place the cursor to the right of the last slide and click on the **Paste** button.

15.   Slides can be moved between presentations in the same way as text. Select the new last slide and click the **Cut** button.

16.   Use the **Taskbar** button to display the **CIA** presentation and select the last slide.

17.   Click on the **Paste** button. The slide from **My Product2** is inserted at the end.

18.   Leave both presentations open.

Driving Lesson 34 - Copy & Paste

🅿 Park and Read

Text, graphics and slides may also be copied. When this action is carried out, the item stays in its original place and a copy of it is placed on the **Clipboard**.

An item that has been cut or copied may be pasted any number of times.

Items can be copied within a slide, between slides, or between presentations.

🔛 Manoeuvres

1. In **Normal View**, select **Our Company** on the **Presentation Agenda** slide. Click on the **Copy** button, 🖺.

ℹ️ *Alternatively use the **Edit | Copy** menu or the key press <**Ctrl C**> to copy items.*

2. Look at the **Clipboard** to see that a copy of **Our Company** has been placed there, while the original text has stayed in place.

3. Place the insertion point just after the **s** of **The Products** and press <**Enter**> to create a new bullet and empty line for the copied text to be pasted into. Click on the most recent **Our Company** icon from the **Clipboard** to paste the copied text into the slide at the new location.

ℹ️ *The **Paste** button, 🖺, or the key press <**Ctrl V**> can be used to paste the last item cut or copied.*

4. If a new line is not started automatically, press <**Enter**> again to start one and click the **Paste** button. The copied text is pasted again.

ℹ️ *The **Paste Smart Tag**, 🖺, can appear and be used in exactly the same way as with cutting and pasting.*

5. Delete the last two insertions of **Our Company**.

6. Use <**Backspace**> to remove all unnecessary blank bullet lines from the list. Remove any extra space.

7. Close the **Clipboard**.

8. Change to **Slide Sorter View** and click on the **Presentation Agenda** slide, slide **2**.

Driving Lesson 34 - Continued

9. Now click on the **Copy** button, 🔲.

10. To paste a copy of the slide, place the cursor on the last slide (slide 3) and click on the **Paste** button, 🔲. A copy of the **Presentation Agenda** slide is added to the end of the presentation

11. Use the **Taskbar** to move to the **My Product2** presentation, and in **Slide Sorter View**, place the cursor between slides **1** and **2**.

12. Click 🔲. The slide copied from the **CIA** presentation is pasted into this one. Notice how the current slide design is automatically applied to it.

13. Delete the pasted slide, number **2**.

14. Text can be copied between presentations in the same way. On slide **1**, select the **Title** text and click on the **Copy** button, 🔲.

15. Use the **Taskbar** to move to the **CiA** presentation.

16. Display slide **3** and select the title text. Click the **Paste** button. The title text from the other presentation is pasted in and replaces the original text.

17. In the **CIA** presentation, delete slides **3** and **4**.

18. Close the **My Product2** presentation <u>without</u> saving and leave the **CIA** presentation open.

Driving Lesson 35 - Animation Schemes

🅿 Park and Read

Animation can be applied to text and objects on a slide so they appear on the slide in a variety of different ways, e.g. fly from top, dissolve, etc. Animation schemes exist with preset animation that can be can be applied in 3 possible areas: **Slide Transition** (how does the slide come into the presentation), **Title Animation** (how does the title appear on the screen) and **Body Animation** (how does the rest of the slide appear).

☞ Manoeuvres

1. Show slide **1**, **CIA Training Ltd** in **Normal View**. There is no need to select a particular area as animation schemes apply to the whole slide.

2. Select **Slide Show | Animation Schemes** to display the **Animation Schemes** view of the **Slide Design** task pane

> ℹ️ *To remove animation, select No Animation from the task pane.*

3. Make sure the **AutoPreview** box at the bottom of the pane is checked so that any selected scheme is demonstrated immediately in the **Slide** pane.

4. In the list of animation schemes find **Wipe** and leave the pointer over it. A **ToolTip** appears indicating the effects included in this scheme.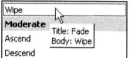

5. Click **Wipe** and the effects of the title fading in and the text wiping from the left will be displayed in the **Slide** pane. All effects are shown, regardless of how they are to be triggered.

6. Click the [🖵 Slide Show] option from the **Slide Design Task Pane** to see how the slide will actually appear. The slide appears immediately and the title fades in, Click with the mouse to trigger the body text. Press **<Esc>** to return to **Normal View**.

> ℹ️ *Animation properties such as triggers, timings and sound are included in some schemes but can only be amended by using the **Custom Animation** feature.*

7. Try out some of the other animation schemes but finally select **Unfold**. This has a **Slide Transition** (**Push Right**) as well as a **Title** effect (**Fly In**) and a **Body** effect (**Unfold**).

> ℹ️ *In **Slide Sorter View** slides with animation are indicated by a star symbol.*

8. Click **Slide Show** to see how the presentation is affected. Remember to click with the mouse where necessary to trigger the next text item.

9. Press **<Esc>** to end the show and return to **Normal View**. Leave the presentation open for the next Driving Lesson.

Driving Lesson 36 - Custom Animation

▣ Park and Read

Custom animation allows effects for individual items to be chosen from 4 areas:

Entrance effects (how an item comes onto the screen),

Emphasis effects (what it does on the screen),

Exit effects (how an item disappears)

Motion Paths (to move an item around a slide).

More than one animation effect can be applied to the same item.

Customising also allows greater control over such details as the timing and order of the animations, the accompanying sound and the appearance of text after animation. For any selected effect, all the options can be set from a dialog box with 3 tabs.

The **Effect** tab controls the addition of sounds, what happens to the item after animation and whether text appears all at once, word by word or letter by letter.

The **Timing** tab controls when an effect is activated - on the click of the mouse or automatically, how fast the effect runs and whether it repeats.

The **Text Animation** tab controls how the effects are applied to a bulleted text list (either to the whole list or by heading/subheading).

⌒ Manoeuvres

1.   In **Normal View** make sure the first (**Title**) slide is selected, then select **Slide Show | Custom Animation**. The **Custom Animation** task pane will be displayed.

2.   The individual animated objects set up by the **Animation Scheme** for this slide are listed in the task pane. Click on the **Title** area of the slide in the **Slide** pane at the right of **Normal View**. The **Title** area is highlighted on the slide and in the list.

3.   Notice the text areas on the slide have numbered boxes showing the sequence in which they will be animated. The sequence is also shown in the list of animation effects in the task pane. Click on the **Re-Order** down arrow to animate the **Title** after the text. Click the up arrow to return the **Title** to the top of the order again.

Driving Lesson 36 - Continued

4. The **Title 1** line in the effects list is already selected, click the **Change** button at the top of the pane and select **Entrance** to see a list of alternative entrance effects. Try out some of the effects and then select **Spiral In** (it may be necessary to select **More Effects** in order to find this effect). Click **OK**.

5. Click the drop down arrow on the **Title 1:** line.

6. Select **Effect Options** to display the dialog box to set all animation controls for the selected effect. Make sure the **Effect** tab is selected.

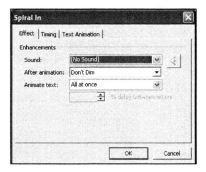

7. Click in the **Sound** box to display the sounds available to accompany the animation. Select a sound if required.

8. Click in the **Animate text** box, and select to introduce the text **By word**.

9. Select the **Timing** tab and look at the options available. Change the **Speed** setting for the effect.

10. Click **OK** in the dialog box to preview the effect that has just been amended.

11. Click the **Play** button in the task pane to preview all the current animation.

12. Experiment with different effects and settings.

13. Save and close the **CIA** presentation.

Driving Lesson 37 - Spell Checking

P Park and Read

A presentation can be checked at any time for spelling errors, including repeated words. The spell checker is the same as that in *Word*, it will suggest alternatives for words it does not recognise; these can be accepted or ignored, or in the case of a repeated word, deleted. Words can be added to the dictionary if desired.

Right clicking on an incorrectly spelled word displays a shortcut menu listing possible alternatives.

Manoeuvres

1. Open the **Marketing** presentation (words spelled incorrectly will be underlined with a red wavy line).

2. Click on the **Spelling** button, to start the spell checker, or select **Tools | Spelling**. The spelling for the whole presentation will be checked.

3. When the **Spelling** dialog box appears, either click **Ignore** to leave the selected word unchanged or click **Change** to replace the word. The word can be replaced by selecting one from the **Suggestions** list or by typing a new word into the **Change to** box.

i *If necessary, the dialog box can be moved to see the context of the word before making a selection from **Suggestions**. Just click and drag the box by its blue **Title Bar**.*

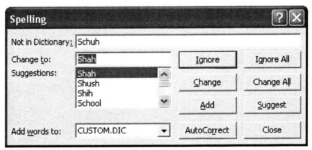

4. When finished spell checking, click **OK** (if any mistakes were corrected or repeated words deleted). Close the **Spelling** dialog box, if necessary.

5. Leave the presentation on screen for the next Driving Lesson.

Driving Lesson 38 - Master Pages

▣ Park and Read

Master pages contain text or graphics that are to be displayed on every page of a presentation. There are four master pages: **Slide**, **Title**, **Handout** and **Notes**, which act as templates, to allow consistent formatting, text and graphics to be applied to the slides, notes and handouts accompanying the presentation.

↱ Manoeuvres

1.   Using the **Marketing** presentation, click on slide **1**. Select **View | Master | Slide Master**. The **Title Master** and **Slide Master** are shown in the left pane. Select the **Slide Master** (the upper slide) to display it in the main **Slide** pane. Anything put on this slide will appear on every slide except the title slide.

> **i** *This is because the **Theme** applied to this presentation has defined a separate master slide for title slides (Title Master).*

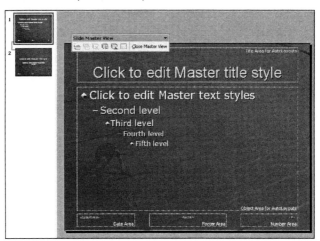

> **i** *The position of the **Slide Master View** toolbar may vary. It can be dragged out of the way if it obscures the slide.*

2.   Click the **Text Box** tool, , on the **Drawing** toolbar and drag the mouse to create a text box on the right side of the master slide, across about three quarters of the width of the slide.

3.   Type **This text appears on every slide except the first**.

                                                                              ☞

Driving Lesson 38 - Continued

4. Select **View | Normal**. The text entered on to the master slide appears on every slide, except the title slide. It may be obscured by other material on the slide - it is always best to create the master slide before adding material to the individual slides.

5. View the **Slide Master** again and click on **Click to edit Master title style**. Format the title so that it is centre aligned, in bold and underlined.

6. Return to **Normal View** - all slide titles now have this formatting applied.

7. Return to the **Slide Master**. To remove the text typed earlier, click on the text to display it then click on the edge of the text box and press <**Delete**>.

8. To insert an imported object (a picture called **Photo** from the supplied data files) to the master slide select **Insert | Picture | From File**.

9. In the **Look in** box of the **Insert Picture** dialog box, locate the folder with the supplied data files. Select the picture **Photo** and then click **Insert**.

> **i**   *If the **Picture** toolbar appears, close it.*

10. Resize the photo by clicking on one of the corners, (the cursor should change to ↘), and dragging inwards, until it is about half its original size.

11. Move it to the bottom right corner by clicking in the centre, (the cursor should change to ⊹), and dragging.

> **i**   *Working with objects in PowerPoint will be covered in more detail in the next Section.*

12. In **Normal View**, notice that the photo has been copied on to every slide in the presentation, except the **Title** slide.

13. To remove the photo, return to the **Slide Master** slide, click on the photo to select it and press <**Delete**>.

> **i**   *All objects (pictures, images, drawn objects) are deleted in this way.*

14. To change the background colour of all slides, select **Format | Background**.

15. Click the drop down arrow at the bottom of the **Background** dialog box and select the green square.

16. Click **Apply** and switch to **Normal View** to see the change. Because the change was applied to the **Slide Master**, all slide backgrounds, apart from the **Title** slide, have changed.

> **i**   *If the **Slide Master** were not being viewed, **Apply** would only change the background of the selected slide. It would be necessary to select **Apply to All**.*

17. Close the presentation <u>without</u> saving.

Driving Lesson 39 - Headers & Footers

◳ Park and Read

Headers and **Footers** are items of information that appear at the top and/or bottom of every slide, or notes and handouts. This information usually consists of the date, the page or slide number and text such as the company name. The date can be fixed or inserted as a field in a number of different formats.

◲ Manoeuvres

1. Open the **CIA** presentation.

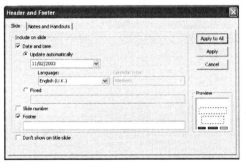

2. To apply a header and footer to slide **1** only, select it in **Normal View**, then select **View | Header and Footer**.

3. Click on the **Slide** tab if not already selected.

4. Place a tick in the **Date and time** checkbox and select to update it automatically.

5. Click on the drop down arrow next to the box displaying the date and choose one of the available formats. The date will always be updated and always in this format.

6. Place a tick in the **Slide number** checkbox so that the slide will be numbered correctly.

7. Choose to have a slide **Footer** and in the text box type **CIA Training Ltd**.

8. Click **Apply** to apply only to the selected slide.

9. Look at slide **2** - there are no headers and footers. Select slide **1** and select **View | Header and Footer**.

10. To stop the date updating automatically select the **Fixed** option from **Date and time** and enter a specific date in the adjacent box. This date will always be shown. Click on **Apply to All** this time to apply the information to all of the slides.

11. Select **View | Header and Footer**, switch to the **Notes and Handouts** tab and select to have **Page numbers** and a **Footer** of **Compliments of CIA Training**. Click on **Apply to All** to apply this to all the notes / handouts.

12. View the slides in **Slide Sorter View**, then in **Notes Page View** to observe the different footers in each view.

13. Save the presentation and close it.

Driving Lesson 40 - Revision

This covers the features introduced in this section. Try not to refer to the preceding Driving Lessons while completing it.

1.   Open the presentation **Welcome**.

2.   Format all of the slide titles to change the text style to **Tahoma**.

3.   Increase the title text size to **48 pt**.

4.   Change the main bulleted text for each of the slides to **20 pt** and make them bold.

5.   Select the subtext on the title master, italicise the text and remove the shadow effect.

6.   On the title master, use the line spacing option to format the bulleted lists on each slide to have **0.5 line spacing** before and after each paragraph.

7.   Select slide **2**, format the bullets using an arrow character of your choice.

8.   Using slide **3** change the bullets to numbers.

9.   Use the **Undo** command to undo the last action.

10. Use the **Redo** command to restore the numbers.

11. On slide **2** select the bullet **Founded in 1985...** and cut it from the list.

12. Paste the text at the bottom of the list as a new bulleted line. Delete any blank bulleted lines that may remain.

13. Create a new **Title and Text** slide at the end of the presentation with a title of **History**.

14. With the **Clipboard** task pane open, copy both the text **Founded in 1985...** from slide **2**, and the third bullet from slide **3**.

15. Paste the last 2 copied items to make 2 bullet points on the **History** slide.

16. Ensure the same bullets are applied to both lines.

17. Run the slide show from slide **1**.

18. Save the presentation as **Welcome2** and close it.

If you experienced any difficulty completing the Revision, refer back to the Driving Lessons in this section. Then redo the Revision.

Driving Lesson 41 - Revision

This covers the features introduced in this section. Try not to refer to the preceding Driving Lessons while completing it.

1.   Open the presentation **Garage** in **Normal View**.

2.   Using **Custom Animation**, apply an **Entrance Effect** of **Stretch** to the title (Grange Garages). For this and every other animation effect in this exercise, set the speed to **Slow** to see the effect more clearly.

3.   Select each car manufacturer's name in turn and apply an **Entrance Effect** of **Fly in**.

4.   Apply the **Entrance Effect** style **Dissolve In** to the **Open Day** text box and the **Finance** text box.

5.   View the slide show. Click the mouse to start each effect.

6.   Using the **Custom Animation** feature again, apply the following effects:

Slide Object	Animation Effect	Sound
Man/car image	Spiral In	Applause
'Address' box	Zoom	Whoosh

7.   Run the slide show.

8.   Save the presentation as **Open Day** and close it.

If you experienced any difficulty completing the Revision, refer back to the Driving Lessons in this section. Then redo the Revision.

Once you are confident with the features, complete the Record of Achievement Matrix referring to the section at the end of the guide. Only when competent move on to the next Section.

Section 4
PowerPoint Objects

By the end of this Section you should be able to:

Insert and Modify an Organisation Chart

Move, Resize and Copy Objects

Insert and Animate Clip Art

Insert a Picture / Chart

Use Drawing Tools and AutoShapes on Slides

Select, Rotate and Flip Objects

Arrange and Distribute Objects

Change Object Colours

Import Images

To gain an understanding of the above features, work through the **Driving Lessons** in this **Section**.

For each **Driving Lesson**, read the **Park and Read** instructions, without touching the keyboard, then work through the numbered steps of the **Manoeuvres** on the computer. Complete **Revision Exercise(s)** at the end of the section to test your knowledge.

Driving Lesson 42 - Organisation Charts

Park and Read

Slides in a presentation are composed of various objects which, although easy to insert, can result in an impressive show. In a company presentation, it is often a good idea to insert an organisation chart to demonstrate the company's structure.

Manoeuvres

1. Open the presentation **CIA** in **Normal View** and insert a new slide after slide **2**.

2. From the **Slide Layout** task pane, scroll down and select the layout **Title and Diagram or Organization Chart**, ⊞.

3. Double click to display the **Diagram Gallery** dialog box. Look at the diagrams available then select the **Organization Chart** and click **OK**.

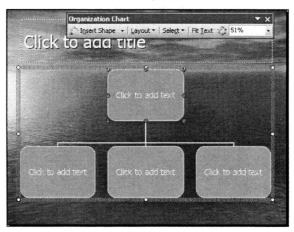

4. Close down the **Task Pane** to give the **Slide** pane more room.

5. Add the slide title **Company Structure** and centre it.

6. Select **Layout** on the **Organization Chart** toolbar and ensure that **AutoLayout** is selected (handles on the top shape in the chart should be as shown above). *PowerPoint* then controls the positioning of the boxes and lines and they cannot be manually moved.

Driving Lesson 42 - Continued

7. Click in the top box and type **Brian Brown,** press **<Enter>** and type **Director**.

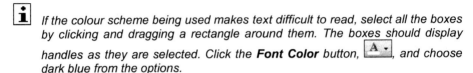 *If the colour scheme being used makes text difficult to read, select all the boxes by clicking and dragging a rectangle around them. The boxes should display handles as they are selected. Click the **Font Color** button, , and choose dark blue from the options.*

8. Click in the left box and enter **Joanne Malone** on the first line and **Training Manager** on the second line.

9. Make the middle box **Katharine Deacon, Quals Supervisor** and the last box **Jean Barker, Office Manager**.

10. Click the box for **Joanne Malone**, click the drop down arrow on **Insert Shape** from the **Organisation Chart** toolbar and select **Subordinate**. A new box is created linked to Joanne's. Click in the new box and enter **Andrew Wilson, Trainer**. Change the **Font Color** for the new boxes if required.

11. Add a co-worker to **Andrew Wilson**, click on **Andrew Wilson** and select **Insert Shape | Coworker**. Add the text **Michael Jones, Trainer**.

12. Add a subordinate to **Jean Barker** named **Lynsey Lightfoot, Clerk**

13. Jean Barker also has an assistant, use **Insert Shape | Assistant** to add a box then enter the details **Neera Singh, Accounts**. Press **<Esc>** to return to **Normal View**

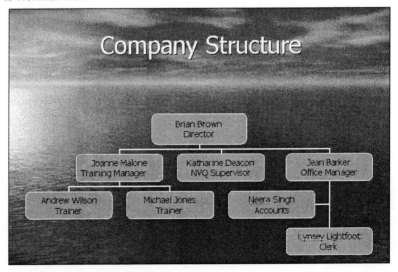

14. Save the presentation and leave it open.

Driving Lesson 43 - Modify Organisation Chart

▣ Park and Read

It may be necessary to move or resize an object after placing it on a slide. All objects can be resized or repositioned so that they occupy the correct amount of space and position.

☞ Manoeuvres

1. With slide **3** in **Normal View**, select the organisation chart by clicking on it once. Handles and a border should appear around it and an **Organization Chart** toolbar will appear somewhere.

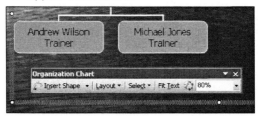

2. Move the mouse pointer over the chart border, click and hold the mouse button down. Drag the chart around the slide (a dotted outline of it should be visible). Release the mouse button.

3. Click and drag the chart handles to resize the chart area.

4. Jean Barker has left and been replaced by Eileen Dover. Select the text **Jean Barker** in the box and replace it with **Eileen Dover**.

5. Michael Jones has left and not been replaced. Click on the edge of the box with his name (make sure the handles appear) and press <**Delete**>. All types of shape can be removed this way.

6. To modify the chart manually, select **Layout** on the **Organisation Chart** toolbar and deselect **AutoLayout**.

7. To change the reporting structure for Andrew Wilson, click on the connecting line to his box. The line will have a red circle at each end.

8. Click and drag the upper red circle across to the bottom edge of the box for Katherine Deacon. The link is repositioned.

9. Click the edge of Andrew Wilson's box (the handles are now white circles) and drag it so that it lines up below Katherine Deacon's.

ⓘ *If **AutoLayout** is switched back on, the boxes (but not the links) will resume their original positions.*

10. Save the presentation and leave it open.

Driving Lesson 44 - Inserting Images

▣ Park and Read

PowerPoint has a useful **Clip Gallery**, where images and symbols can be chosen for insertion on a presentation slide.

ⓘ *The large number of graphics included with Office 2003, means that some of them are stored on the CD and not necessarily installed. If graphics used in the following Driving Lessons are unavailable, either insert the CD, or replace the specified graphic with an alternative. Graphics from other programs can also be incorporated into presentations - providing that they can be imported.*

⌒ Manoeuvres

1. Using the presentation from the previous Driving Lesson, view slide **3** in **Normal View** and use the **New Slide** button to insert a new slide **4**.

2. From the **Slide Layout Task Pane**, scroll down and select a layout named **Title, Text and Clip Art**.

3. Add the slide title **An Example Of Clip Art** and centre it.

4. Double click in the position indicated to add **Clip Art**. The **Select Picture** dialog box is displayed. The contents of the gallery will vary depending on installation and there may be a delay as the images load.

5. Any picture could be selected or specific searches can be made. Enter **cars** in the **Search for** box and click **Go**. Only pictures that meet the search criteria are displayed.

6. Select any picture from those displayed then click **OK**.

7. The picture is now inserted on the presentation slide (the **Picture** toolbar may be displayed).

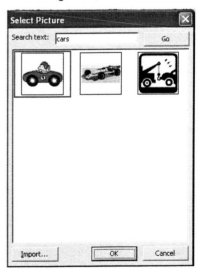

ⓘ *Clip Art placed on the Slide Master will appear on every slide.*

ⓘ *Clip Art can be added to any slide layout using Insert | Picture | Clip Art and selecting to view the Clip Organizer.*
Copy and **Paste** *will be required to insert the pictures onto the slide.*

8. Leave the presentation open.

Driving Lesson 45 - Manipulating Images

🅿 Park and Read

Images can be copied, moved, resized and deleted.

↱ Manoeuvres

1.   The picture will probably already be selected, i.e. have handles visible. If not, click once on it to display the handles.

2.   Practise resizing the picture by clicking and dragging on the handles. Click and drag the corner handles to maintain the correct proportions of the picture.

3.   Hold down the **<Ctrl>** key and then click and drag one of the handles. This time, the picture is resized about its centre.

4.   Practise moving the picture. Hold down the **<Shift>** key as the picture is dragged to move the image either horizontally or vertically.

5.   Select the picture and click on the **Copy** button, 📋, then **Paste**, 📋, to create another copy of the picture on the same slide.

6.   To delete the copied picture, click on it and then press **<Delete>**.

7.   To move the original image to another slide, select the image and click on the **Cut** button, ✂.

8.   View slide **2** and click on the **Paste** button, 📋, to place the image on this slide.

9.   Delete this slide from the presentation by switching to **Slide Sorter View** and selecting **Edit | Delete Slide**.

10. View the third slide in **Normal View** and from the menu select **Format | Slide Layout**. Select the **Title Only** layout and change the slide title to **New Clip Art**.

11. Now click on **Paste** to paste the picture on to this slide.

12. Open the **Garage** presentation and insert a new blank slide and click 📋 to paste the image to this presentation.

ℹ️   *Images can be copied <u>or</u> moved between presentations in this way.*

13. Close the **Garage** presentation <u>without</u> saving and leave the **CIA** presentation open for the next Driving Lesson.

Driving Lesson 46 - Animating Images

🄿 Park and Read

Animation effects have been applied to text earlier, but they can also be applied to images.

⟳ Manoeuvres

1. With slide **3** of the presentation on screen select the clip art image by clicking on it.

2. To animate the image, select **Slide Show | Custom Animation** and click the **Add Effect** button in the **Custom Animation Task Pane** and select the **Entrance** option.

3. Select the **Crawl In** effect (it may be necessary to select **More Effects** and click **OK** first).

4. From the boxes in the **Custom Animation Task Pane** select a direction of **From Right** and a speed of **Very Slow**.

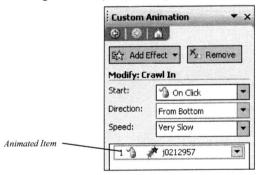

5. Click the **Play** button to see the effect.

6. To change the animation effect, select the **Animated Item** from the list, click the **Change** button and make a new selection. Click **Play** to see the effect.

7. Select animation **1** in the **Custom Animation** task pane and click **Remove**, [Remove] to delete it.

8. Save the presentation and leave it open for the next Driving Lesson.

Driving Lesson 47 – Tables

▣ Park and Read

There are various ways to present data in *PowerPoint*. Tables often provide a clearer way than text to present numerical data.

🖰 Manoeuvres

1. Create a new slide at the end of the presentation. Scroll down the **Slide Layout** pane and click on the **Title and Table** layout to select it.

2. Enter the title **Sales Table** and double click where indicated on the slide to insert a table.

3. From the **Insert Table** dialog box, select **4** columns and **2** rows.

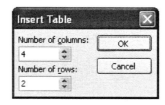

4. Click **OK** and enter the following data into the table, pressing **<Tab>** to move from cell to cell, or **<Shift Tab>** to move back a cell.

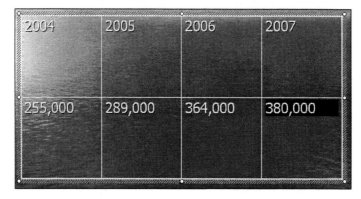

2004	2005	2006	2007
255,000	289,000	364,000	380,000

5. There is more data to add to the table. To insert a new row, click in the second row. From the **Tables and Borders** toolbar, click Table ▾ and then select **Select Row**.

6. Click Table ▾ again and select **Insert Rows Above**.

Driving Lesson 47 - Continued

7. Using the middle handle at the bottom of the table, drag it up until it fits on the slide again.

8. In the new row **2**, enter the following figures: **350,000**, **439,000**, **424,000** and **475,000**.

9. These figures don't make much sense. A column must be inserted at the left. Click in the left column. Select **Table | Select Column** and then **Table | Insert Columns to the Left**.

10. Again, resize the table to fit the slide.

11. In row **1** of the new column, enter **Year**. Below, enter **Turnover** and on the bottom row, **Profit**.

12. Edit the **2005 Turnover** figure **439,000** to **389,000** by clicking on the cell and making the change.

Year	2004	2005	2006	2007
Turnover	350,000	389,000	424,000	475,000
Profit	255,000	289,000	364,000	380,000

13. Move the mouse over the row divider between rows **1** and **2** until it becomes ⬍. Click and drag up to reduce the height of the row. Repeat this for the other rows.

14. Use the same method to resize the column widths to fit the text neatly.

15. It has been decided that the **2004** column is no longer required. Click in the column and then **Table | Delete Columns** to remove it.

ℹ️ *Rows are removed in a similar way by selecting the row/s and then* **Table | Delete Rows**.

16. There is probably a better way to present data like this. Click on the table border to select the whole table and then press **<Delete>**.

17. Delete the slide and leave the presentation open for the next Driving Lesson.

Driving Lesson 48 - Spreadsheets

Park and Read

Spreadsheets are probably a better way to present data like this. A spreadsheet file can be inserted directly into a presentation.

Manoeuvres

1. Create a new, **Title Only** slide at the end of the presentation.

2. Click to add the slide title **Spreadsheet Extract**.

3. To insert data from a spreadsheet, first select **Insert | Object**.

4. From the **Insert Object** dialog box, select **Create from file** and click **Browse**.

5. Locate the data files and select the file **Sales.xls** (make sure **Files of type** shows **All Files**).

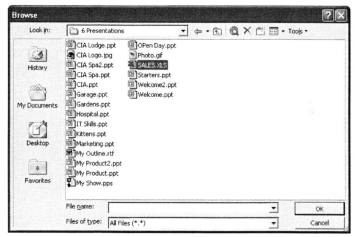

6. Click **OK** and then **OK** in the **Insert Object** dialog box to insert the spreadsheet extract.

7. Save the presentation and leave it open for the next Driving Lesson.

Driving Lesson 49 - Charts

▣ Park and Read

You can insert charts into a presentation. Sometimes a chart makes figures easier to understand.

☞ Manoeuvres

1. Create a new slide at the end of the presentation. Scroll down the **Slide Layout Task Pane** to find the **Title Text and Chart** layout. Click to select it. This slide has room for text on the left and a chart on the right.

2. Enter the slide title **CiA Sales of Guides** and double click where indicated on the slide to insert a chart.

ℹ️ *A chart can be inserted on to a slide with a different layout by, clicking the* ***Insert Chart*** *button,* 📊*, on the toolbar.*

3. *Microsoft Graph* then starts, displaying a new menu and toolbar and a sample datasheet on the screen. A sample chart, based on the datasheet is also shown on the slide.

▦ CIA.ppt - Datasheet		A	B	C	D	E
		1st Qtr	2nd Qtr	3rd Qtr	4th Qtr	
1 ▫	East	20.4	27.4	90	20.4	
2 ▫	West	30.6	38.6	34.6	31.6	
3 ▫	North	45.9	46.9	45	43.9	
4						

4. This datasheet can be edited to the user's specification by changing figures, titles, etc. Rows and columns can be added or removed. In the datasheet, click on the word **East** and overtype it with **Word**.

5. Replace **West** with **Excel** and **North** with **Access** then press **<Enter>**.

6. The default chart is a **Clustered column with a 3-D visual effect**. To change the **Chart Type**, select **Chart | Chart Type** to display the **Chart Type** dialog box.

ℹ️ *Alternatively, clicking on the drop down arrow of the **Chart Type** button,* 📊▾*, on the toolbar, will display a reduced list of available types from which to choose.*

Driving Lesson 49 - Continued

i *The **Chart** menu and the **Chart Type** button are only available when a chart is selected for editing, i.e. double clicked.*

7. From the **Standard Types** tab, click on each chart type in turn. A list of each chart's sub-types is displayed on the right hand side. Preview how the chart will appear by selecting a sub-type and holding down the
    | Press and Hold to View Sample | button.

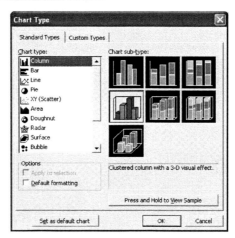

8. Select the first sub type of the **Column** chart and click **OK**.

9. Click on the slide, away from the chart datasheet, to place the chart on the slide.

i *To select a chart, click once on it.*

10. Double click on the chart to edit it. If the datasheet is not visible click on the **View Datasheet** button, 🖽. Change the **Word** figures for the **1st Quarter** from **20.4** to **40**. Observe the change, which is reflected immediately in the chart.

11. Close the datasheet by using its **Close** button or click the **View Datasheet** button.

12. Click in the text pane on the left and add the bulleted text:

    - Sales for last year
    - Analysed by Product
    - Figures in Thousands

13. Leave the presentation open for the next exercise.

Driving Lesson 50 - Formatting Charts

▣ Park and Read

The appearance of all parts of a chart can be changed using the buttons on the **Chart** toolbar or by selecting **Chart | Chart Options**. These options are only available when a chart is selected for editing.

↱ Manoeuvres

1. There are various buttons on the **Chart** toolbar used for changing the appearance of a chart.

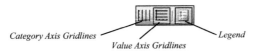

    Category Axis Gridlines —————   ————— *Legend*
    Value Axis Gridlines

2. If the chart does not have vertical (**Category Axis**) gridlines, add them by clicking the ⊞ button, or by selecting **Chart | Chart Options | Gridlines** and selecting an option from the dialog box. Click **OK**.

3. Position the mouse pointer somewhere over the chart. A **ToolTip** will appear to indicate which feature of the chart is selected. Use this method to locate the **Plot Area**, which is the back wall of the chart, not on a gridline.

4. Double clicking on any part of the chart displays the formatting dialog box for that area. With the **Plot Area** selected, double click to display the **Format Plot Area** dialog box.

5. Change the colour of the area by clicking on a pale yellow square from the selection of colours on the right side of the dialog box and clicking on **OK**. Experiment with other back wall colours and use some of the available **Fill Effects**.

ℹ️ *This method of double clicking on any part of a chart is used to change the colour of lines, pie slices and bars in the different chart types.*

6. Use the **ToolTip** to locate the **Word data series** (any of the data columns for Word). Right click and select **Format Data Series** to display the **Format Data Series** dialog box. Change the colour of the columns to red or some other suitable colour.

7. Double click on the horizontal axis to display the **Format Axis** dialog box. Click on the **Font** tab and change the font to **Times New Roman** in **Bold Italics**. Click **OK**.

8. Leave the presentation open for the next exercise.

Driving Lesson 51 - Adding Chart Labels

▣ Park and Read

Titles can be added to charts to identify specific areas. You can also add data labels to show values, numbers or percentages. Data labels show the precise value of each data series in the chart.

Manoeuvres

1. At the end of the presentation insert a new **Title and Chart** slide with the title **Bar chart** and double click to add the chart.

    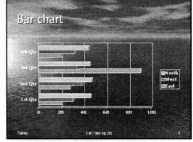

2. Select **Chart | Chart Type** and the first **Bar chart** sub type on the second line. Click **OK**. The chart is added and will be automatically selected.

3. Select **Chart | Chart Options** and the **Data Labels** tab. Select the **Value** option.

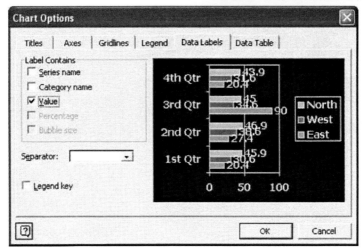

4. Select the **Titles** tab. Enter the chart title **Regions** in the area provided. Click **OK**.

5. The chart title is to be edited. Select **Chart | Chart Options** and on the **Titles** tab, change the chart title to **UK Regions**. Click **OK**.

Driving Lesson 51 - Continued

6. In fact, a title is not needed; click on the title to select it. Press **<Delete>** to remove it.

7. Click away from the chart to place the chart on the slide.

8. Insert a new **Title and Chart** slide at the end of the presentation. This time change both the title and chart type to **Line chart** (first sub type).

9. Place the chart on the slide.

10. Create a final chart on a new slide, this time selecting a **Pie chart** (second sub type) and change the slide title as appropriate. Place the chart on to the slide.

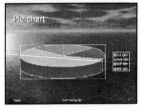

11. To add data labels, select the chart, select **Chart | Chart Options** and the **Data Labels** tab.

12. This time select **Percentage** and click **OK**.

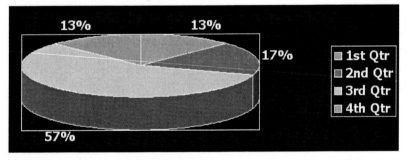

13. To format an individual segment, first make sure the chart is in **Edit** mode then click on the 'pie' to select all segments.

14. Click on the green slice to select that individual segment then select **Format | Selected Data Point**.

15. Change the colour of the area by clicking on a red square from the selection of colours on the right side of the dialog box and clicking on **OK**.

16. From the **Slides pane** in **Normal View**, click on the **Bar chart** slide to select it and then hold down the **<Shift>** key.

17. Still holding down **<Shift>**, click on the **Pie chart** slide. Three chart slides are now selected. To delete these new slides, press **<Delete>**.

18. Save the changes to the presentation and leave it open for the next Driving Lesson.

Driving Lesson 52 - Drawing & Objects

Park and Read

The **Drawing** toolbar allows drawings to be made directly on to a slide. The **Drawing** toolbar can only be displayed in **Normal View** and **Notes Pages View**. The buttons relating to drawing are:

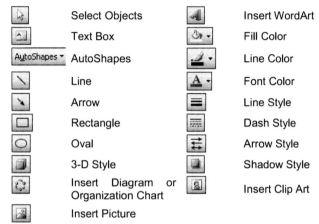

	Select Objects		Insert WordArt
	Text Box		Fill Color
AutoShapes ▾	AutoShapes		Line Color
	Line		Font Color
	Arrow		Line Style
	Rectangle		Dash Style
	Oval		Arrow Style
	3-D Style		Shadow Style
	Insert Diagram or Organization Chart		Insert Clip Art
	Insert Picture		

Objects can be drawn by clicking on the appropriate button and then clicking and dragging on the slide. All objects have **handles**, similar to clip art, that can be used to reshape and re-size the drawing.

Manoeuvres

1. Using the **CIA** presentation, create a new, **Title Only**, slide after the existing slides and enter the title **Drawing**.

2. Select **View | Toolbars | Drawing** to display the **Drawing** toolbar (usually along the bottom), if it is not already on view.

3. Click the **Line** button, ⬕, then click and drag a line on the slide.

4. In a similar way, draw a rectangle anywhere on the slide.

> **i** *Holding down <**Shift**> while drawing an oval will create a circle or, while drawing a rectangle, will produce a square.*

5. To draw a freeform line, click, AutoShapes ▾, then select **Lines** and click **Freeform**, ⬚. Click and hold down the mouse and drag to create a curving line. Double click to complete the freeform line.

6. Practise drawing lines, rectangles, squares, arrows, circles and ovals (ellipses). Draw a block arrow from **AutoShapes**.

> **i** *Drawn objects placed on the **Slide Master** will appear on every slide.*

Driving Lesson 53 - Formatting Drawn Objects

▣ Park and Read

The **Drawing** toolbar allows changes to be made to drawn objects by using the buttons on the **Formatting** toolbar. Objects are selected by simply clicking on them. Selected objects display their handles.

Manoeuvres

1. Click on an **oval** on the **Drawing** slide. It displays handles when selected.

2. Click on the drop down arrow on the **Fill Color** button, [icon]. Choose a different colour from the options. Change the line colour by clicking on the drop down arrow on the **Line Color** button, [icon] and selecting a colour.

3. Now select a rectangle, then click the **Shadow Style** button, [icon].

4. From the grid displayed, use **Tooltips** to find **Shadow Style 4**.

5. Click the button to apply the shadow.

6. Click and drag to move the rectangle - the shadow moves with it.

7. Click on a line and change its thickness by clicking on the **Line Style** button, [icon] and choosing from the one of the options.

8. With the line still selected, click and drag to move it around on the slide.

9. Change the line to an arrow, select it and click **Arrow Style**, [icon].

10. Choose the **Arrow Style 3** option.

11. The start and end style of arrows can be changed. Make sure the arrow line is selected and click [icon] again. Select **More Arrows**.

12. From **End style** within the **Arrows** area, choose the **Oval Arrow**.

13. Click **OK** to apply the style to the arrow.

14. Right click on a square and select **Add Text** from the shortcut menu. A cursor flashes in the shape. Alternatively, just click inside the shape. Type your first name. Click outside the shape to complete the process.

15. In the same way, add your name to a block arrow, a rectangle, an oval and a circle. Leave the presentation open for the next Driving Lesson.

Driving Lesson 54 - Rotate or Flip Objects

▣ Park and Read

Any drawn object can be rotated or flipped.

↰ Manoeuvres

1.   On the **Drawing** slide select **AutoShapes | Basic Shapes**.

2.   Click on the **Heart** shape, then click and drag on the slide to draw a heart. As well as the white sizing handles each object has a green **Rotate** handle.

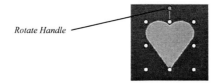

Rotate Handle

3.   Move the mouse pointer over the **Rotate** handle of the heart and click and drag. The object rotates about the centre.

4.   Try rotating the object whilst holding down **<Shift>**. The object rotates in fixed steps of 15 degrees.

5.   Try rotating the object whilst holding down **<Ctrl>**. The object pivots about the opposite sizing handle.

6.   Select **Draw | Rotate or Flip | Free Rotate** from the **Drawing** toolbar. The single **Rotate** handle disappears and all corners of the object become **Rotate** handles and can be manipulated as above. Click away from the object to switch off these handles.

7.   Select or draw an oval.

8.   Rotate the oval so it is at an angle, like in the diagram below:

9.   To flip the oval, select **Draw | Rotate or Flip | Flip Vertical**.

10. Try rotating and flipping some other objects. Flipping symmetrical objects such as circles and squares will not produce any visible effects. Leave the presentation open for the next Driving Lesson.

Driving Lesson 55 - Manipulating Objects

🅿 Park and Read

Click and drag an object to move it around a slide, or cut and paste it to move it between slides, or to a different presentation.

Click and drag the handles of any object to change its size.

Objects can also be copied within a presentation or to another one.

🗘 Manoeuvres

1. Move to the **Chart** slide and click once on the chart to select it. To resize the chart, click on the top right handle. Click and drag inwards to reduce the size of the chart.

2. Use the same handle to click and drag outward until the chart is its original size.

3. Click in the centre of the chart and drag it to a new position on the slide.

4. Move it back to its original position.

5. With the chart still selected, click 🔖 to remove it. Open the **Marketing** presentation and create a new blank slide at the end.

6. To move the chart to this presentation, click 🔖.

7. The chart should be selected, if not click on it once. Press <**Delete**> to delete it.

8. Use the **Taskbar** to move to the **CIA** presentation and the **Chart** slide. Click 🔖 to replace the chart in its original position.

9. Now click 🔖 to duplicate the chart (notice the original is untouched).

10. Create a new blank slide at the end of the presentation and click **Paste** to copy the chart here.

11. Move back to the **Marketing** presentation, and select the last slide.

12. Paste the chart again, then delete it and move back to the **CIA** presentation. Select the **Drawing** slide and select any square/rectangle.

Driving Lesson 55 - Continued

13. Resizing and moving is the same for all objects. Click and drag a corner handle outward to make the object bigger.

14. With the object selected, click the **Cut** button, ![cut icon], move to the **Marketing** presentation, select the blank last slide and click ![paste icon] to paste the drawn object.

15. Select and then delete the object in the same way as deleting a chart.

16. Move back to the **CIA** presentation and the **Drawing** slide. Select any drawn object.

17. Copy it, then paste it into the blank slide at the end of the **Marketing** presentation.

18. Close the **Marketing** presentation without saving and leave the **CIA** presentation open.

Driving Lesson 56 - Arranging Objects

⊞ Park and Read

Objects on a slide can be moved around the slide either individually or as a group. They can be moved so that they overlap each other, much like pieces of overlaying paper. This can allow complex shapes and effects to be built up, but care must be taken to ensure that important information is not covered up.

When overlapping, the order of objects in the 'stack' can be changed if necessary, by moving them backward or forward.

Manoeuvres

1. Using the **Drawing** slide, click on any object. Press **<Shift>** and select another object. Both objects should now be selected and any formatting will be applied to both objects. Click and drag a corner handle on one of the objects, both objects will be equally resized. Click away to deselect them.

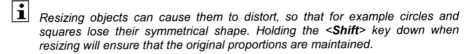 *Resizing objects can cause them to distort, so that for example circles and squares lose their symmetrical shape. Holding the **<Shift>** key down when resizing will ensure that the original proportions are maintained.*

2. Click on the **Select Objects** button, . Click and drag around a few objects. A dotted rectangle appears until the mouse button is released. Any shapes wholly within the rectangle will be selected.

3. Move one shape slightly to the left - all of the selected objects move. Click away from the objects to deselect them.

4. Arrange several of the objects on the slide so that they are **on top** of each other.

5. Select the object that is on top of the others. Click the **Draw** button and point to **Order**.

6. Select **Send to Back** from the list displayed. The object will now be **under** the others.

7. Select **Draw | Order | Bring to Front** to bring the object back to the top.

8. Practise using the **Back/Front** and **Forward/Backward** options within **Draw | Order** to rearrange objects. Notice the difference between bringing an object <u>forward</u> and bringing it to the <u>front</u>.

Driving Lesson 56 - Continued

9. Delete all objects on the slide and draw a square, a circle and an oval. Move them to random positions similar to that shown below.

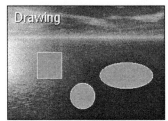

10. To align the objects to the top of the slide, first select them all.

11. Select **Draw | Align or Distribute** and make sure that **Relative to Slide** is selected.

12. Select **Align Top** from the **Draw | Align or Distribute** menu. All the objects are aligned with the top of the slide.

[i] *If **Relative to Slide** had not been selected, the objects would be aligned with the top edge of the highest of the objects.*

13. To align the objects to the right, select **Draw | Align or Distribute | Align Right**. The objects are now on top of each other because they have not been distributed.

14. Select **Draw | Align or Distribute | Distribute Vertically**. The objects are distributed evenly over the vertical edge of the slide.

15. Use the **Align or Distribute** command to align the objects to the left of the slide.

16. Now align them at the bottom of the slide and then distribute them horizontally.

17. Finally, use **Align Middle** to line up the objects across the middle of the slide.

[i] *Any objects, i.e. drawn objects, **Clip Art** pictures, or images from file can be manipulated in this way.*

18. Click away from the objects to deselect them.

Driving Lesson 57 - Grouping Objects

▣ Park and Read

Objects can be grouped; this allows them to be treated as a single object.

⌒ Manoeuvres

1. Click on the object at the left. To group the objects, hold down **<Shift>** and click on the others in turn.

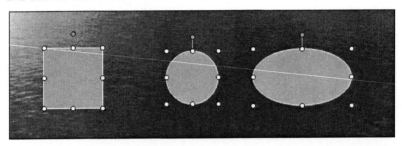

2. Click the **Draw** button and select **Group**.

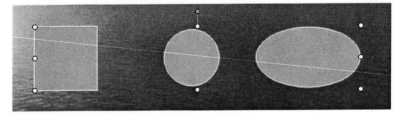

3. Move one object - notice how they all move.

4. Use the single green rotate handle to rotate the grouped objects.

5. Rotate the group back to their original position.

6. Click **Draw** again and then select **Ungroup** to separate the objects. They can now be manipulated individually.

7. Deselect the objects.

8. Leave the slide on screen.

Driving Lesson 58 - Colours and Lines

▣ Park and Read

Drawn objects (including text boxes) can have the colour of their lines and fills changed. The style of the line may also be changed.

↱ Manoeuvres

1. To begin changing the lines and fill colours, either double click on the object to be formatted or right click and select **Format AutoShape**. Using the **Drawing** slide from the previous Driving Lesson, double click on any of the objects on the slide.

2. The **Format AutoShape** dialog box appears with the **Colors and Lines** tab to the front. Click on the **Fill** box to reveal the drop down menu. Select a colour.

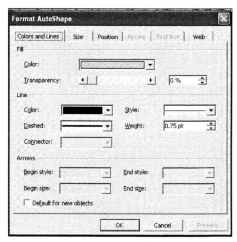

3. Change the **Transparency** setting to **50%**, ether by using the slider or the value box, then click **OK**. Move the object over the title, **Drawing** - the text should be visible underneath the shape.

4. Drag the object away from the title and double click on the object again and drop down the **Fill** colours again.

5. Select **Fill Effects** and view the various effects available from each of the tabs before choosing one of the available **Texture** options.

6. Click **OK** to return to the **Format AutoShape** dialog box.

7. Change line type, colour, style, weight and dash effects then click **OK**.

8. Leave the presentation on screen for the next Driving Lesson.

Driving Lesson 59 - Importing Images

🅿 Park and Read

Images can be imported into *PowerPoint* from other files.

♟ Manoeuvres

1. Using the presentation **CIA**, create a new blank slide at the end of the presentation ready to accept an imported picture.

2. To import an image from a file, select **Insert | Picture | From File**.

3. The file called **CIA Logo** can be found in **My Documents\CIA DATA FILES\ECDL\6 Presentations**, click on the name.

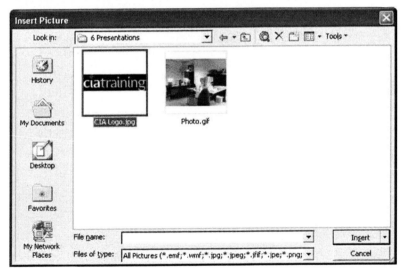

ℹ️ *The **Insert Picture** dialog box can appear in many different views, which can be selected using the **Views** button,* ⊞▾. *The view shown here is **Preview**.*

4. Click **Insert**.

5. The image should be placed on the new slide and can then be enlarged and repositioned by clicking and dragging, the same as any other object.

6. Save the presentation and close it.

Driving Lesson 60 - Revision

This covers the features introduced in this section. Try not to refer to the preceding Driving Lessons while completing it.

1. Using a new, blank presentation, start a new slide based on an organisation chart, with the title **Little Town F.C.**.

2. Create the chart below:

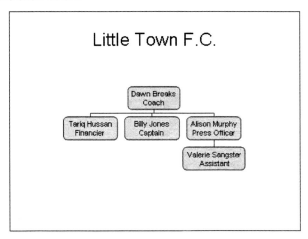

3. Now modify it to produce this chart layout:

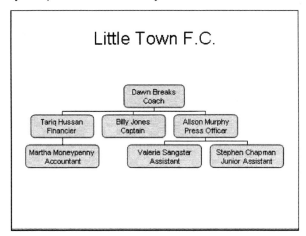

Driving Lesson 60 - Continued

4.   Create a new slide based on a **Blank** layout.

5.   Select Insert | Picture | Clip Art and select a picture from the Clip Gallery.

6.   Place it on the slide. Insert a second image.

7.   **Copy** and **paste** one of the images, within the same slide.

8.   **Resize** one of the images.

9.   Create another new slide based on a **Chart**.

10. Give it a title and then double click on the chart icon to enter *Microsoft Graph*.

11. Use the information in the datasheet, but change the chart type to a **pie chart**.

12. This chart is not appropriate for the data. Change the chart type to a **Clustered column with 3-D visual effect**.

13. Change the colour of the chart walls (**Walls**) to light blue and the area around the chart (**Plot Area**) to green.

14. Change the **colours** of the three data series to any colour scheme desired.

15. On a new blank slide import the image with the filename **Pyramid**. Re-size as required.

16. Create another new blank slide and produce some **drawings** using the features on the **Drawing** toolbar.

17. Save the presentation as **Examples** and close it.

If you experienced any difficulty completing the Revision, refer back to the Driving Lessons in this section. Then redo the Revision.

Driving Lesson 61 - Revision

This covers the features introduced in this section. Try not to refer to the preceding Driving Lessons while completing it.

1. Create a new blank presentation using the **Title and Table** layout.

2. Insert the title **Victoria's Wine Sales - Table**.

3. Insert a table with **5** columns & **4** rows.

4. Enter the information shown below into the table. Use the **<Tab>** key to move to the next cell when the data for a cell has been entered. Use **<Tab>** with **<Shift>** held down to move back one cell. Click in any cell to edit the data there:

	January	February	March	Total
Red	120	112	143	375
White	280	247	228	755
Rose	98	90	87	275

5. Change the column widths if necessary to achieve the appearance above. Click and drag the borders between the columns to do this.

6. Insert a column for **April** in the appropriate place. Enter the following figures: **Red 172, White 250, Rose 103**.

7. Click away from the table to place it on the slide.

8. Create a new **Title and Chart** slide, where a column chart is to be created. Enter the title **Victoria's Wine Sales - Chart**.

9. Using the data in the table above, retype the figures into the datasheet. Do not include the **Total** column, but replace it with the following figures for **April**: **Red 172, White, 250, Rose, 103**.

10. Click away from the chart to place it on the slide.

11. Add data labels showing **values**.

12. Save the presentation as **Wine Sales**.

13. Close the presentation.

If you experienced any difficulty completing the Revision, refer back to the Driving Lessons in this section. Then redo the Revision.

Driving Lesson 62 - Revision

This covers the features introduced in this section. Try not to refer to the preceding Driving Lessons while completing it.

1. Create a new presentation using the **Title Only** layout.

2. Add the title **Office Layout**.

3. Draw a large rectangle underneath the title and change the fill colour to represent the floor.

4. Draw an oval that covers the title and order so that the text can be seen.

5. Change the fill colour of the oval to dark blue.

6. Change the text colour to white.

7. Select **Autoshapes | More AutoShapes** to open a **Task Pane** containing many small clip art images, including some which can be used for creating room layouts.

8. Create an office layout according to the following instructions. Moving, rotating and resizing of objects will be required.

9. Place a desk along the west (left) wall of the office.

10. Place a chair next to the desk.

11. Insert a 3-seater couch and a circular table and place in the top right hand corner of the room.

12. Add a door swing in the middle of the south wall of the room and a file cabinet in the middle of the north wall.

13. Insert a plant on the round table and a telephone and PC on the desk.

14. Select the rectangle and add a 3pt black line.

15. Save the presentation as **Layout**.

16. Close the presentation.

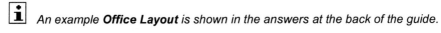

An example **Office Layout** *is shown in the answers at the back of the guide.*

If you experienced any difficulty completing the Revision, refer back to the Driving Lessons in this section. Then redo the Revision.

Once you are confident with the features, complete the Record of Achievement Matrix referring to the section at the end of the guide. Only when competent move on to the next Section.

Section 5
Slide Shows

By the end of this Section you should be able to:

Select the Correct Output Format

Set up a Slide Show

Apply Slide Transitions

Run the Presentation

Print Slides, Presentations and Handouts

To gain an understanding of the above features, work through the **Driving Lessons** in this **Section**.

For each **Driving Lesson**, read the **Park and Read** instructions, without touching the keyboard, then work through the numbered steps of the **Manoeuvres** on the computer. Complete the **Revision Exercise(s)** at the end of the section to test your knowledge.

Driving Lesson 63 - Output Format

▣ Park and Read

A presentation can be given using different methods, such as on an overhead projector, an on-screen show, or just as handouts for the audience. The output format should be selected before the presentation is run.

↱ Manoeuvres

1. Open the presentation **Hospital**. The presentation is to be shown on an overhead projector. Select **File | Page Setup**.

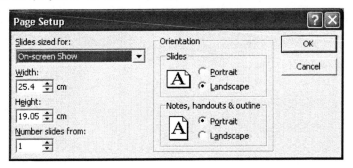

2. The presentation is currently set up as an **On-screen Show**. Click on the drop down list for **Slides sized for**.

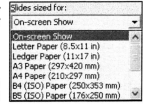

3. Select **Overhead** and click **OK**.

4. Select **File | Page Setup** and change the size setting to **A4 Paper** and click **OK**. This would be used to print handouts of the slide show.

5. From the **Page Setup** dialog box, change the size to **Letter Paper**.

6. Click **OK**. The slide image changes slightly to indicate how it would look when printed on **Letter** size paper.

7. From the **Page Setup** dialog box, select the **Custom** size option. The size of the slide can now be defined using the **Height** and **Width** boxes. Set a height of 20cm and a width of 10cm and click **OK** to see the effect.

8. Now change the slide size format back to **On-screen show** so that it reverts to its original size. Leave the presentation open.

Driving Lesson 64 - Slide Design

▣ Park and Read

The slide setup, e.g. the slide orientation may be changed, as well as the orientation of the **Notes Pages**, **Handouts** and **Outlines**.

↱ Manoeuvres

1. Use the presentation **Hospital**.

2. To change the orientation of the slides in the presentation, select **File | Page Setup**.

3. Select **Portrait** for **Slides Orientation**, then click **OK**. The slide orientation changes.

Landscape   *Portrait*

ℹ️ *Within the **Page Setup** dialog box there is also an option to separately change the orientation of the **Notes, handouts and outline** pages.*

4. Return the slide orientation to **Landscape**.

Driving Lesson 65 - Setting up a Slide Show

▣ Park and Read

The following Driving Lessons demonstrate how to set up the show, with transitions and timings, etc.

⌐ Manoeuvres

1. With the **Hospital** presentation in **Normal View** and the **Slide** pane on the left, select **Slide Show | Set up Show**. The following dialog box appears.

2. Make selections in the dialog box opting for **Show type** set to **Presented by a speaker**, **Show slides** set to **All** and **Advance slides** set to **Manually**.

3. Click **OK**.

4. Select either **Slide Show | View Show** or **View | Slide Show,** to start the slide show with the first slide in the presentation. This would not necessarily be slide 1 if a range of slides had been specified in **Show slides**.

[i] *Clicking the **Slide Show** button, [⌨], will start the slide show from the currently selected slide whereas **View Show** menu command always starts with slide 1.*

5. Click the mouse to move to the second slide. Change the mouse pointer to the **Ballpoint Pen** using the **Pointer Options** menu. Use the pen to draw on this slide.

6. Move through the rest of the slide show and at the end, click to exit opting to keep annotations and return to **Normal View**. Leave the presentation open.

Driving Lesson 66 - Slide Transition

▣ Park and Read

A **transition** is a special effect that controls how one slide changes to the next. It refers to the whole slide whereas **animation** applies to the individual text or objects on a slide.

↷ Manoeuvres

1. In **Normal View**, click on the **Title** slide of the **Hospital** presentation.

2. Select **Slide Show | Slide Transition**.

3. Scroll down the list of transition effects shown in the **Task Pane**. Make sure the **AutoPreview** box is checked and pick any effect. A demonstration of the effect is shown.

4. Try using some of the other effects to see what they do.

5. Select the effect **Newsflash**, click on the speed **Medium**, select some sound if required and make sure the **On mouse click** box is checked. The **Title** slide now has its transition effect defined and has a star symbol next to it in the **Slides** pane to indicate this.

6. Click on the second slide and choose a different transition from the list.

7. Apply transition effects to the rest of the slides (use **Apply to All Slides** if the same transitions are to be used on each slide).

 To remove a transition, select No Transition from the task pane.

8. Select the first slide then click on the **Slide Show** button to run the slide show. Click the mouse button to move from one slide to the next.

9. Select the first slide in **Slide Sorter View**.

10. To change the transition, select the **Wedge** effect from the **Slide Transition Task Pane** with a **Medium** speed and select to **Apply to All Slides**.

11. Run the slide show to see the new effects.

12. Save the presentation as **Transitions** and close it.

Driving Lesson 67 - The Presentation

🅿 Park and Read

Assume that the **CIA Training Ltd**. presentation is now complete. All that remains now is to practise slide navigation and then to print the slides, handouts and notes, etc.

🢌 Manoeuvres

1. Open the **CIA** presentation.

2. The slides in the presentation are to be advanced manually using the mouse button. Alter the settings in the **Set Up Show** dialog box so that the slide timings are disabled.

3. The **Slide Show** button, 🖵, starts the slide show from the currently selected slide. To start the presentation with the third slide, missing out slides **1** and **2**, select the third slide before clicking 🖵 to start the slide show.

4. Press <**Esc**> to end the show. Slide **5** is not to be viewed during this presentation, hide it by selecting the slide first and then clicking on **Slide Show | Hide Slide**. Notice the icon in the **Slides** pane, ⑤.

5. Run the show from slide **1** and notice that slide **5** will not appear.

6. To view slide **5** in future presentations, select the slide, then select **Slide Show | Hide Slide** to switch off the feature.

ℹ️ *Initially, the presentation should run in slide order. The slide navigation tools (accessed by right clicking during the slide show) are mainly used when the presenter is asked questions and needs to display non-adjacent slides. The tools can be used to go to the **Next**, **Previous**, **Last Viewed** slide, or to a specific slide number.*

7. Run the show again from slide **1**, but do not move on.

8. Move the mouse pointer to the bottom left hand corner of the slide and click the button which appears to display the **popup menu**.

9. View the slide options and select **Go to Slide**.

10. Select slide **5**. The show will jump to that slide.

11. Display the popup menu again, and explore the other options.

12. Exit the show by pressing <**Esc**> and leave the presentation open.

Driving Lesson 68 - Printing

▣ Park and Read

In *PowerPoint* you can print out slides, notes pages, outlines and handouts in various formats. When printing slides, there is the choice of whether to print **All** the slides, just the **Current** slide or just the specified **Slides**.

Manoeuvres

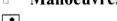

*To preview the slides before printing, change to **Slide Sorter View**.*

1. In any view, select **File | Print** or the key press **<Ctrl P>**, the **Print** dialog box is displayed.

2. Check that the printer is ready to print. If the printer shown at the top of the dialog box is incorrect, click on the **Printer Name** text box and select the correct one.

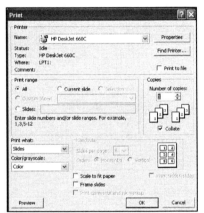

3. From **Print what**, select **Slides**. From **Copies** and **Print range** respectively, opt to print **1** copy of **All** slides, then click **OK**.

4. To print two copies of a single slide, select slide **1**.

5. Select **File | Print** and from **Print range** select **Current slide**. Select **2** from **Number of copies** and click **OK**.

6. To print slides 2 to 4 only, select **File | Print** and from **Print range** select **Slides**. Type **2-4** in the **Slides** box and click **OK**.

7. Select **File | Print**. From **Print what** select **Handouts**. The **Handouts** section of the dialog box becomes active. Set **Slides per page** to **4**.

8. Notice that there are also options to print the handouts horizontally or vertically. Click **OK**.

9. Select **File | Print** and use the **Print what** box to print **Notes Pages** and then **Outline View**.

*If you do not have access to a printer the presentation can be printed to a file instead. Select **File | Print** and check **Print to file**. Click **OK** and enter a **File name** in the **Print to File** dialog box. Click **Save**.*

10. Close the presentation, saving the changes.

Driving Lesson 69 - Revision

This covers the features introduced in this section. Try not to refer to the preceding Driving Lessons while completing it.

1.   Open the presentation **Gardens**.

2.   Apply a design of your choice to the slides.

3.   Change the orientation to **portrait**.

4.   Set up and run the slide show.

5.   Apply a different transition to each slide.

6.   Print one of the slides.

7.   Start the presentation on the second slide, with the last slide hidden.

8.   Save the presentation as **Garden2** and close it.

9.   Open the presentation **Kittens**.

10.   Apply a different transition effect to all of the slides.

11.   Run the slide show.

12.   Print out the current slide.

13.   Print out handouts showing **4** slides per page.

14.   Save the presentation as **Cats**.

15.   Close the presentation.

16.   Close *PowerPoint*.

If you experienced any difficulty completing the Revision, refer back to the Driving Lessons in this section. Then redo the Revision.

Once you are confident with the features, complete the Record of Achievement Matrix referring to the section at the end of the guide.

Answers

Driving Lesson 10

Step 6   A toolbar contains buttons which are used to access the most common menu commands.

Step 15   Preferences are basic option settings.

Step 17   This will vary between computers but typically 6 or 8.

Step 18   There are **12** items on the full **Slide Show** menu.

Driving Lesson 11

Step 45   a) **New Slide**

b) **Print**

c) **Open**

d) **Save**

e) **New**

f) **Microsoft PowerPoint Help**

Driving Lesson 62

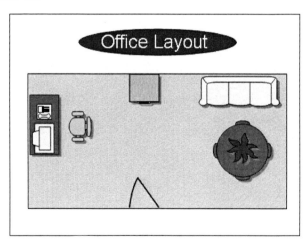

Glossary

Alignment The arrangement of text or objects in relation to the slide or text box, e.g. left, centre, right, top, bottom.

Animation Special effects which make text and other objects appear to move on screen.

Animation Scheme A collection of animation effects which can be applied to a slide with a single selection.

Arrange Position overlapping objects in relation to each other. They can be brought forward or sent backward, placed on the top or bottom of the pile.

Background The colour of the slide.

Copy Create a duplicate of an object or text. Used when the copied item is to be duplicated.

Custom Animation Applying animation effects to individual objects on a slide and specifying their operation.

Cut Remove an object or text. Used when the cut item is to be moved somewhere else.

Design Template *PowerPoint* contains many of these pre-set designs for slides. Applied to all slides.

Flip Move an object as if it is reflected, e.g. left becomes right, or top becomes bottom.

Footer Text or numbers appearing at the bottom of the slide, notes page or handout.

Formatting Changing the appearance of text, graphics, etc.

Header Text or numbers appearing at the top of the slide, notes page or handout.

Import Bring a file into a presentation from another application.

Object Item on a slide, e.g. drawn shape, image, chart, text box.

Orientation Which way up the slide/handout is: **Portrait** or **Landscape**.

Output Format How the presentation is to be given, e.g. on screen or using an overhead projector.

Page Setup Allows the size and orientation of slides to be changed.

Glossary

Paste	Used after **Cut** or **Copy** to position the item (move or duplicate).
Preferences	Basic program settings, which can be changed.
Presentation	A collection of slides used by a speaker as a visual aid.
Rotate	Move an object clockwise or anticlockwise about its axis.
Save	Keep a permanent copy of your work on the hard or floppy drive of the computer.
Slide Layout	The type of slide, e.g. **Bulleted List**, **Title Only**, **Chart and Text**, etc.
Slide Master	This view is for adding items that are to appear on all slides in a presentation.
Slides	Make up the presentation, each refers to a specific area.
Slide Show	A preview of the presentation, with all effects, sounds, etc.
Text Effects	Formatting such as bold, italic, shadow, superscript.
Toolbars	Contain buttons (icons) to perform tasks quickly.
Transition	How one slide moves to the next.
Views	Different ways of looking at slides.

Index

Record of Achievement Matrix

This Matrix is to be used to measure your progress while working through the guide. This is a learning reinforcement process; you judge when you are competent.

Tick boxes are provided for each feature. 1 is for no knowledge, 2 some knowledge and 3 is for competent. A section is only complete when column 3 is completed for all parts of the section.

For details on sitting ECDL Examinations in your country please contact the local ECDL Licensee or visit the European Computer Driving Licence Foundation Limited web site at http://www.ecdl.com.

Tick the Relevant Boxes **1**: No Knowledge   **2**: Some Knowledge   **3**: Competent

Section	No	Driving Lesson	1	2	3
1 Getting Started	1	Starting PowerPoint			
	2	The PowerPoint Screen			
	3	Presentations			
	4	Menus			
	5	Toolbars			
	6	Help			
	7	The Office Assistant			
	8	Preferences			
	9	Closing PowerPoint			
2 Slides & Presentations	12	Views			
	13	Slide View			
	14	Outline View			
	15	Slide Sorter View			
	16	Notes Page View			
	17	Slide Show			
	18	Saving a Presentation			
	19	Closing a Presentation			
	20	Opening Presentations			
	21	New Presentations			
	22	Creating a Presentation			
	23	Adding and Deleting Slides			
	24	Changing Slide Layout			
	25	Background Colour			
3 Formatting	28	Formatting: Font & Size			
	29	Undo and Redo			
	30	Applying Text Effects			
	31	Alignment, Spacing & Case			
	32	Bullets			
	33	Cut & Paste			
	34	Copy & Paste			

Tick the Relevant Boxes 1: No Knowledge   2: Some Knowledge   3: Competent

Section	No	Driving Lesson	1	2	3
3 Formatting (continued)	35	Animation Schemes			
	36	Custom Animation			
	37	Spell Checking			
	38	Master Pages			
	39	Headers & Footers			
4 PowerPoint Objects	42	Organisation Charts			
	43	Modify Organisation Chart			
	44	Inserting Images			
	45	Manipulating Images			
	46	Animating Images			
	47	Tables			
	48	Spreadsheets			
	49	Charts			
	50	Formatting Charts			
	51	Adding Chart Labels			
	52	Drawing & Objects			
	53	Formatting Drawn Objects			
	54	Rotate or Flip Objects			
	55	Manipulating Objects			
	56	Arranging Objects			
	57	Grouping Objects			
	58	Colours and Lines			
	59	Importing Images			
5 Slide Shows	63	Output Format			
	64	Slide Design			
	65	Setting Up a Slide Show			
	66	Slide Transition			
	67	The Presentation			
	68	Printing			

Other Products from CiA Training Ltd

CiA Training Ltd is a leading publishing company, which has consistently delivered the highest quality products since 1985. A wide range of flexible and easy to use self teach resources has been developed by CiA's experienced publishing team to aid the learning process. These include the following ECDL Foundation approved products at the time of publication of this product:

- **ECDL/ICDL Syllabus 5.0**

- **ECDL/ICDL Advanced Syllabus 2.0**

- **ECDL/ICDL Revision Series**

- **ECDL/ICDL Advanced Syllabus 2.0 Revision Series**

- **e-Citizen**

Previous syllabus versions also available - contact us for further details.

We hope you have enjoyed using our materials and would love to hear your opinions about them. If you'd like to give us some feedback, please go to:

www.ciatraining.co.uk/feedback.php

and let us know what you think.

New products are constantly being developed. For up to the minute information on our products, to view our full range, to find out more, or to be added to our mailing list, visit:

www.ciatraining.co.uk